I0522008

I Will Not Have "Pun" in Class!

2nd Edition

TIMOTHY "SMITTY" SMITH

Published by Timothy "Smitty" Smith 2023

ISBN 979-8-9884227-2-3 (paperback)
ISBN 979-8-9884227-3-0 (digital)

Printed in the United States of America

Timothy "Smitty" Smith grew up being a jokester since the age of eight.

Ever since that young age, he has always attempted to find humor in everyday conversations and life with family and friends. He is a man who loves to joke and is a master at "a play on words" type of humor. Once you get his style, you get his humor.

His goal for everyone who reads and hears his material is to "think outside the norm" of the original meaning of a word or phrase. Sometimes, it requires a little more thought, but once you get one joke, you should get most of them; and he hopes it will brighten everyone's day who reads his material.

So sit back, relax, and open his book of jokes and puns and enjoy his humorous world along with him because one thing we all need today is more humor and laughter!

Smittionary

"Not your ordinary dictionary"

To get the best effect, say the
italicized word(s) slowly

Smittionary
"Not your ordinary dictionary"
To get the best effect, say the italicized word(s) slowly

A

Word: abatement

True definition: a deduction from the full amount of a tax

My definition: a lower level of a house or building

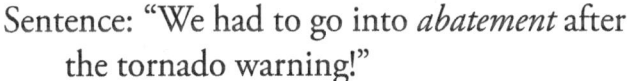

Sentence: "We had to go into *abatement* after the tornado warning!"

Word: acme

True definition: highest point

My definition: the act of someone getting information from you

Sentence: "Why didn't you just *acme*? I would have told ya!"

Word: according

True definition: statedly or following

Smittionary
"Not your ordinary dictionary"
To get the best effect, say the italicized word(s) slowly

My definition: the sound a brand of car makes when you leave the keys in the ignition!

Sentence: "Keys left in the ignition is why you hear that *according* noise!"

Word: accrue

True definition: to periodically gain interest

My definition: people that you hang around or that work for you

Sentence: "Let me get *accrue* together, and we will be able to do the job for you!"

Word: alyssum

True definition: a plant believed to cure rabies

My definition: to write down items on paper

Sentence: "My concerns? I think *alyssum* from one to ten."

Word: Alzheimer's

True definition: a disease of the brain affecting memory

My definition: tools belonging to Alt used to drive nails

Sentence: "Can I borrow *Alzheimer's* to build a birdhouse?"

Smittionary
"Not your ordinary dictionary"
To get the best effect, say the italicized word(s) slowly

Word: adept
True definition: thoroughly proficient
My definition: immersing in water or liquid
Sentence: "It was hot today, so *adept* in the
    pool for a minute!"

Word: abrupt
True definition: involving change without
    warning or preparation
My definition: noise coming from my mouth
    after drinking a carbonated drink
Sentence: "*Abrupt*, but I did say excuse me!"

Word: actin
True definition: cellular protein
My definition: It's what you tell your twelve-
    year-old to do at a ten-and-under-eat-
    free restaurant!
Sentence: "I need you to *actin* today because
    I'm a little short on funds!"

Word: adduct
True definition: to bring together similar
    parts (as in the fingers)
My definition: It's the answer I got when I
    asked the man what he did when a bird
    flew over his head.

Smittionary
"Not your ordinary dictionary"
To get the best effect, say the italicized word(s) slowly

Sentence: "What did you do when the bird flew over your head?" He said, '*Adduct*!'"

Word: administer
True definition: to distribute or hand out
My definition: what you do to a pastorless church!
Sentence: "We have the choir, the church, and the musicians. Now all we have to do is to *administer*!"

Word: Adonis
True definition: a youth loved by Aphrodite
My definition: something I've experienced before
Sentence: "I really think *Adonis* last year!"

Word: affiliated
True definition: closely associated
My definition: blaming a man for eating something
Sentence: "You said your whole pie is missing and George was the only one in here? *Affiliated*!"

Word: affluent
True definition: flowing in abundance

Smittionary
"Not your ordinary dictionary"
To get the best effect, say the italicized word(s) slowly

My definition: It's where you took a plane to.

Sentence: "*Affluent* to Miami at seven o'clock this morning!"

Word: affront

True definition: to cause offense

My definition: calling someone out that is fake

Sentence: "They don't have a lot of money! It is just *affront*!"

Word: aforethought

True definition: previously in mind

My definition: thinking of the number after three

Sentence: "After thinking of nothing but threes, I finally had an *aforethought*."

Word: afro

True definition: a seventies hairstyle

My definition: how far I can pitch an item

Sentence: "*Afro* the ball pretty far, don't I?"

Word: agape

True definition: being in a state of wonder

My definition: a piece of fruit used to make wine

Smittionary
"Not your ordinary dictionary"
To get the best effect, say the italicized word(s) slowly

Sentence: "Here at the winery, to your left, you will see *agape* vine!"

Word: aghast
True definition: struck with terror
My definition: to fill up your car
Sentence: "When the prices dropped, *aghast* up my ride and was ready to roll!"

Word: agonize
True definition: to cause to suffer
My definition: an uncooked breakfast food thrown in someone's face
Sentence: "You should have ducked! Now you have *agonize*, your nose, and your ears!"

Word: agony
True definition: intense pain of mind or body
My definition: uncooked breakfast item thrown lower on a person
Sentence: "You got *agony* also!"

Word: airborne
True definition: off the ground
My definition: if your mom delivered you on a plane

Smittionary
"Not your ordinary dictionary"
To get the best effect, say the italicized word(s) slowly

Sentence: "Seven pounds six ounces delivered at thirty thousand feet! You were *airborne!*"

Word: Alaska
True definition: a state in the US
My definition: to request an answer from a female
Sentence: "Do you think Judy wants to go?"
"I don't know. *Alaska.*"

Word: albeit
True definition: although
My definition: volunteering to start off a game of tag
Sentence: "Wanna play tag? *Albeit* first!"

Word: album
True definition: a round plastic record consisting of multiple songs
My definition: to request an item or favor
Sentence: "Your car is down. How are you going to get to the game?"
"I don't know. *Album* a ride from somebody!"

Word: alimony
True definition: spousal support

Smittionary
"Not your ordinary dictionary"
To get the best effect, say the italicized word(s) slowly

My definition: rich, like a famous boxer

Sentence: "Dude, you are loaded! You got *alimony*!"

Word: aliteracy

True definition: the ability to read but not interested in doing so

My definition: animal babies

Sentence: "I counted twelve kittens! Your cat had *aliteracy*!"

Word: allied

True definition: coming together for a common cause

My definition: admitting you told a fib

Sentence: "Okay, you got me! *Allied* about the car!"

Word: alligator

True definition: a reptile found in Florida with many teeth

My definition: alerting your sister or another female of a phone call or someone at the door

Sentence: "Hold on, *alligator* for you!"

Smittionary
"Not your ordinary dictionary"
To get the best effect, say the italicized word(s) slowly

Word: aloe vera

True definition: an extract from a plant used in skin creams

My definition: greeting your friend named Vera

Sentence: "Why, *aloe vera*. How are you today?"

Word: Amish

True definition: colony of people with traditional ways

My definition: a way of telling someone you haven't seen them in awhile

Sentence: "When are you coming back? *Amish* you!"

Word: ammonia

True definition: liquid made from nitrogen and hydrogen

My definition: letting someone know that you know their game

Sentence: "*Ammonia* little scheme, and you won't get away with it!"

Word: Amorite

True definition: a person that lives in Syria

My definition: trying to get someone to agree with you

Smittionary
"Not your ordinary dictionary"
To get the best effect, say the italicized word(s) slowly

Sentence: "I think that it has stopped raining for a while! *Amorite* or wrong?"

Word: anagram
True definition: words made from rearranging the letters of other words
My definition: measurement for drugs
Sentence: "He was caught with a pound of marijuana *anagram* of cocaine!"

Word: anatomy
True definition: the structural makeup of an organism or person
My definition: to confirm a type of insect (gnat)
Sentence: "No, it's not a fly. It looks like *anatomy!*"

Word: ancestor
True definition: a descendent or relative from ways back
My definition: a title for a woman of the church
Sentence: "Brother Smith will welcome the visitors, *ancestor* Smith will read the announcements this morning!"

Smittionary
"Not your ordinary dictionary"
To get the best effect, say the italicized word(s) slowly

Word: asbestos

True definition: fireproof material

My definition: giving something a good try

Sentence: "Well, that's *asbestos* I can do for it!"

Word: aspen

True definition: a type of tree

My definition: If a donkey went to school, this is what he would write with!

Sentence: "In Donkey School, an ass pencil and an *aspen* would be required!"

Word: asphyxia

True definition: lack of oxygen

My definition: a doctor's promise to help you

Sentence: "I see you skinned your knee. Sit still and *asphyxia* right up!"

Word: asset

True definition: sufficient property to pay debts

My definition: a pair of donkeys

Sentence: "Hey, George! Take that *asset* to the barn, please!"

Word: assimilate

True definition: to take into the mind and thoroughly comprehend

Smittionary
"Not your ordinary dictionary"
To get the best effect, say the italicized word(s) slowly

My definition: admitting that you are tardy

Sentence: "What? I was supposed to be here an hour ago? Well, *assimilate* once again!"

Word: associate

True definition: a partner or coworker

My definition: food consumption for women

Sentence: "I fixed her food for her *associate* it all!"

Word: asterisk

True definition: a symbol used to mark a footnote

My definition: taking a chance on something

Sentence: "I know your stock lost money, but *asterisk* you take sometimes!"

Word: asylum

True definition: a facility that cares for the destitute and sick

My definition: the purpose of retail salesperson

Sentence: "I have some good wallets, and *asylum* real cheap!"

Smittionary
"Not your ordinary dictionary"
To get the best effect, say the italicized word(s) slowly

B

Word: baloney

True definition: pretentious nonsense

My definition: method of measurement for dress or skirt to make sure it is not too short!

Sentence: "I always buy my skirts *baloney* so they won't be too short!"

Word: balsa

True definition: a tree that produces a very light but strong wood

My definition: standing up for yourself with a pushy person

Sentence: "No, you can't make me. You're not the *balsa* me!"

Word: Baltimore

True definition: a city in Maryland

17

Smittionary
"Not your ordinary dictionary"
To get the best effect, say the italicized word(s) slowly

My definition: to spend more money

Sentence: "Well, I shopped a little longer, so I *Baltimore* clothes I didn't need!"

Word: Baltimore Orioles

True definition: flock of a species of birds and a baseball team

My definition: purchasing more cookies

Sentence: "I love chocolate cookies with créme filling, so I *Baltimore Orioles*!"

Word: Barbados

True definition: a tourist spot in the West Indies

My definition: a popular girl's doll

Sentence: "I want Santa to bring me three *Barbados* and one Ken doll!"

Word: bareback

True definition: to ride a horse without a saddle

My definition: return of a grizzly

Sentence: "Which way you gonna run? That *bareback* again!"

Word: barley

True definition: ingredient in beer and food

Smittionary
"Not your ordinary dictionary"
To get the best effect, say the italicized word(s) slowly

My definition: hardly or difficultly

Sentence: "I am getting tired. I can *barley* keep my eyes open!"

Word: Barnstable

True definition: city on Cape Cod

My definition: a place where Thelma Lou eats dinner sometimes!

Sentence: "Andy, will you help me set *Barnstable* for dinner, please?"

Word: bayou

True definition: a marshy body of water

My definition: talking to someone to get their opinion

Sentence: "Hey, let me run something *bayou*!"

Word: beeline

True definition: to go quickly on a straight course

My definition: catching people fibbing

Sentence: "He said he met the queen, and I don't believe him 'cause he *beeline* all the time!"

Word: Beirut

True definition: city of Lebanon

Smittionary
"Not your ordinary dictionary"
To get the best effect, say the italicized word(s) slowly

My definition: a famous baseball player

Sentence: "Do you think *Beirut* was the greatest baseball player?"

Word: beneficent

True definition: providing acts of kindness

My definition: a man's sport using poles and hooks and bait

Sentence: "I didn't catch anything even though I *beneficent* all day!"

Word: benign

True definition: not cancerous

My definition: what you be after you be eight

Sentence: "I know you are eight years old now, but on your birthday, you will *benign*!"

Word: bias

True definition: using personal judgement

My definition: It's what your kids ask you constantly in the store.

Sentence: "Will you *bias* this and *bias* that?"

Word: bitter

True definition: tart, tangy, unpleasant taste or a foul mood

Smittionary
"Not your ordinary dictionary"
To get the best effect, say the italicized word(s) slowly

My definition: It's what the dog did to the woman.

Sentence: "She teased the dog, so he *bitter*!"

Word: bitumen

True definition: asphalt used in ancient times for cement and mortar

My definition: That same dog that bit the woman did this.

Sentence: "Two guys teased the same dog, so the dog *bitumen* also!"

Smittionary
"Not your ordinary dictionary"
To get the best effect, say the italicized word(s) slowly

C

Word: cannibal

True definition: one who eats human flesh

My definition: questioning a guy's ability to bowl

Sentence: "He has his own monogrammed ball, but *cannibal?*"

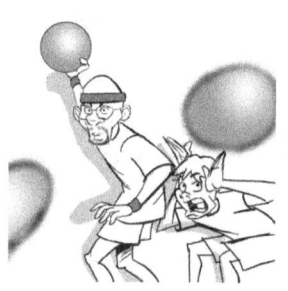

Word: cantaloupe

True definition: a melon with seeds

My definition: telling someone they cannot run off to get married

Sentence: "Everyone wants to be at your wedding, so you "*cantaloupe!*"

Word: carcinoma

True definition: cancer of certain tissues

My definition: another name for a drive-in movie theatre

Smittionary
"Not your ordinary dictionary"
To get the best effect, say the italicized word(s) slowly

Sentence: "When you were little, you called the drive-in the *carcinoma!*"

Word: centimeter
True definition: metric measurement
My definition: picking up a female at the airport
Sentence: "I am looking for Mrs. Jones. Her flight has arrived, and I was *centimeter!*"

Word: cistern
True definition: large storage tank for rainwater
My definition: trying to tell your sister how to drive
Sentence: "The street is coming up on your right. *Cistern* now!"

Word: cognac
True definition: brandy for drinking
My definition: a very talkative prisoner
Sentence: "I wish he would shut up! I been listening to that *cognac* all day!"

Smittionary
"Not your ordinary dictionary"
To get the best effect, say the italicized word(s) slowly

D

Word: debate
True definition: to argue in a formal way
My definition: what a fisherman shouldn't be without
Sentence: "I brought all the fishing poles. Did you remember to bring *debate*?"

Word: decent
True definition: proper or respectable
My definition: the smell of something
Sentence: "Wow! *Decent* of that candle is somewhat overwhelming!"

Word: decompose
True definition: to rot
My definition: trying to take a picture of your friend named Dee

Smittionary
"Not your ordinary dictionary"
To get the best effect, say the italicized word(s) slowly

Sentence: "I got the camera ready. Hey, *decompose* for this picture!"

Word: deduce
True meaning: to lead away
My definition: an older Buick Electra 225
Sentence: "For an older car, he had *deduce* looking pretty good!"

Word: defenseman
True definition: a player in a sport opposite the offense player
My definition: the man who installs your fence
Sentence: "I want a privacy fence, so tomorrow, I'll call *defenseman*!"

Word: defer
True meaning: to put off or delay
My definition: animal-skin outerwear or coat
Sentence: "It is really cold outside, so I think I'll wear *defer* tonight to dinner!"

Word: defiant
True meaning: an act of refusal
My meaning: a very small red biting insect
Sentence: "I think *defiant* bit me on the hand!"

Smittionary
"Not your ordinary dictionary"
To get the best effect, say the italicized word(s) slowly

Word: deficiencies

True definition: shortages

My definition: the swimmers with fins that you can catch, cook, and eat!

Sentence: "I bet you can't count all the different varieties of *deficiencies* and oceans worldwide!"

Word: dehumanize

True definition: to deprive of human qualities

My definition: the parts of the body used for vision

Sentence: "Did you know *dehumanize* possibly blink around fifty times a day?"

Word: denial

True definition: contradiction

My definition: a river in Egypt

Sentence: "One day, I would like to visit *denial* river!"

Word: discontented

True definition: not happy or satisfied

My definition: allowing a prisoner to tint your car windows

Smittionary
"Not your ordinary dictionary"
To get the best effect, say the italicized word(s) slowly

Sentence: "I saved a lot of money today because *discontented* all my windows for twenty-five dollars!"

Word: disguise
True definition: to make unrecognizable
My definition: where you look up and see the clouds and sun
Sentence: "Believe in your dreams because *disguise* the limit for what you want to do!"

Word: disorient
True definition: to confuse
My definition: house payment
Sentence: "I got to pay *disorient* on the first of the month!"

Word: disperse
True definition: to scatter
My definition: what women keep personal items in
Sentence: "Some purses are fake, but *disperse* is authentic leather!"

Word: distinct
True definition: not alike or separate

Smittionary
"Not your ordinary dictionary"
To get the best effect, say the italicized word(s) slowly

My definition: to smell bad

Sentence: "At first, I thought *distinct*, but after a while, the cologne smelled better!"

Word: docket

True definition: list of cases to be tried in court

My definition: what you do to a boat

Sentence: "After we had fun in the boat all day, I pulled it in to *docket*."

Word: document

True definition: written record relied on as evidence

My definition: clarification from your physician

Sentence: "Hey, *document* to prescribe me sixty pills and not forty pills, didn't you?"

Word: during

True definition: throughout or in the course of

My definition: what the best man keeps until needed

Sentence: Pastor: "Okay, who has *during*?"

Word: dynamite

True definition: explosives

Smittionary
"Not your ordinary dictionary"
To get the best effect, say the italicized word(s) slowly

My definition: an alternative choice

Sentence: "I don't think Ann will go to the mall with me, but *dynamite* go!"

Smittionary
"Not your ordinary dictionary"
To get the best effect, say the italicized word(s) slowly

E

Word: ecology

True definition: science related to the interrelationship of organisms and their environment

My definition: a letter called at a bingo game

Sentence: "If *ecology* 45, then I've got bingo!"

Word: Egypt

True definition: a country bordering the Mediterranean and the Red Seas

My definition: getting swindled

Sentence: "Don't buy anything from that salesman! *Egypt* me out of twenty dollars!"

Word: endeavor

True definition: a serious determined effort

My definition: usually is stated between *forever* and *amen*

Smittionary
"Not your ordinary dictionary"
To get the best effect, say the italicized word(s) slowly

Sentence: "Forever *endeavor*. Amen!"

Word: endocardial
True definition: within the heart
My definition: It's when you get fed up with a car salesman at the dealership.
Sentence: "That's not the price we agreed on, so I just want to *endocardial* right now!"

Word: endogenous
True definition: produced by growth from deep tissue
My definition: someone avoiding you and your crew
Sentence: "There's no sense *endogenous* because we know where you live!"

Word: endorse
True definition: to sign the back of a check
My definition: opposite of outdoors
Sentence: "It's getting dark outside, so you kids need to come *endorse* now!"

Word: enduring
True definition: lasting
My definition: where boxers have their match

Smittionary
"Not your ordinary dictionary"
To get the best effect, say the italicized word(s) slowly

Sentence: "Both fighters have now arrived *enduring*!"

Word: Enoch
True definition: a patriarch in the Bible
My definition: someone pounding on your door
Sentence: "I hate salesmen! *Enoch* on my door for ten minutes!"

Word: ensemble
True definition: a group of supporting people
My definition: trumped-up charges
Sentence: "I didn't do nothin'! They arrested me *ensemble* crap!"

Word: eradicate
True definition: to pull up by the roots
My definition: asking your friend Kate to hurry up
Sentence: "It's time to go now. *Eradicate*?"

Word: erect
True definition: vertical in stature as with a building
My definition: traffic mishap

Smittionary
"Not your ordinary dictionary"
To get the best effect, say the italicized word(s) slowly

Sentence: "He just bought that new car, and *erect* it already!"

Word: erector
True definition: a trademark name of a metal building toy
My definition: traffic mishap number two
Sentence: "He is just a bad driver 'cause he drove his wife's car and *erector* car too!"

Word: Erlanger
True definition: a city in Kentucky
My definition: a guy named Earl with a terrible attitude
Sentence: "Boy, is he really mad about that traffic ticket! He's got *Erlanger*!"

Word: erode
True definition: to diminish or destroy by degrees
My definition: past tense of riding
Sentence: "He must be a true cowboy because *erode* that horse like a pro!"

Word: escalator
True definition: motorized moving steps
My definition: future questioning of a woman

Smittionary
"Not your ordinary dictionary"
To get the best effect, say the italicized word(s) slowly

Sentence: "I was gonna ask Judy a question. But I don't see her, so I'll *escalator*!"

Word: escargot
True definition: a delicacy edible snail
My definition: the speed of an automobile
Sentence: "I know it doesn't look fast, but *escargot* 180 miles per hour!"

Word: Eskimo
True definition: a native of Alaska
My definition: further inquiry
Sentence: "I am not satisfied with his answers so far, so I think I will *Eskimo* questions!"

Word: essay
True definition: a report written from your point of view
My definition: something your parents told you as a kid
Sentence: "Don't do as I do. Do as *essay*!"

Smittionary
"Not your ordinary dictionary"
To get the best effect, say the italicized word(s) slowly

F

Word: fancier
True definition: one who has a
    special liking or interest
My definition: bodyguard secu-
    rity issue
Sentence: "The female star fired
    her bodyguard because he let one *fancier*
    house!"

Word: farsighted
True definition: able to see a great distance
My definition: reports of flames and smoke
Sentence: "Call 911 and tell them there's a
    farsighted in the woods!"

Word: faucet
True definition: a fixture for regulating water
    flow
My definition: not real

Smittionary
"Not your ordinary dictionary"
To get the best effect, say the italicized word(s) slowly

Sentence: "It was funny when Grandpa pulled out his *faucet* of teeth!"

Word: fedora
True definition: a type of hat
My definition: a popular kid's cartoon
Sentence: "All the kids are quiet and sitting still in front of the TV *fedora* the explorer!"

Word: federate
True definition: to join in an alliance
My definition: giving food to a rodent
Sentence: "The store owner was mad because his son *federate* some cheese!"

Word: felonies
True definition: crimes punishable with jail time
My definition: falling forward
Sentence: "The man just *felonies* tomatoes and squashed them!"

Word: fluorinate
True definition: to combine with fluoride
My definition: consuming your food sitting on the carpet

Smittionary
"Not your ordinary dictionary"
To get the best effect, say the italicized word(s) slowly

Sentence: "I had the table cleared off, but everyone sat on the *fluorinate*!"

Word: flyswatter
True definition: a device for killing insects
My definition: an insect's drink
Sentence: "The clear liquid in that small glass is the *flyswatter*. They get thirsty too!"

Word: foamy
True definition: consisting of foam material
My definition: belonging to or a favor to you
Sentence: "I am touched because you did this all *foamy*!"

Word: forgetful
True definition: failure to remember
My definition: unfairness
Sentence: "Eight people qualified, but only *forgetful* benefits!"

Word: forgettable
True definition: likely to be forgotten
My definition: leaving behind a dish
Sentence: "You took four bowls but brought back three. Did you *forgettable*?"

Smittionary
"Not your ordinary dictionary"
To get the best effect, say the italicized word(s) slowly

Word: foyer
True definition: a lobby or entryway
My definition: a favor or gift for someone
Sentence: "Hey, come and see me when you get a chance. I got something *foyer* kids!"

Word: freakish
True definition: abnormal or strange
My definition: a no-cost peck on the lips or jaw
Sentence: "The woman at the booth is giving one *freakish* per guy at this year's carnival!"

Word: freaky
True definition: abnormal
My definition: a no-cost lock-opening device
Sentence: "If you buy two keys, you will get one *freaky* with every purchase!"

Word: freon
True definition: gas or liquid used in air conditioning
My definition: no cost on a certain day
Sentence: "I like this restaurant because they let kids eat *freon* Thursdays!"

Smittionary
"Not your ordinary dictionary"
To get the best effect, say the italicized word(s) slowly

Word: frijole

True definition: Mexican cooking bean

My definition: sacred water

Sentence: "The pastor was giving out *frijole* water to his members after the service!"

Word: frill

True definition: edging used on clothing or fabric

My definition: confirmation

Sentence: "What? You won the lottery. Are you *frill?*"

Word: froze

True definition: solid state from liquid

My definition: seventies hairstyle

Sentence: "After using the pick, they got their *froze* looking good!"

Word: furlong

True definition: a distance equal to 220 yards

My definition: short length of time

Sentence: "They better hurry up because I can't stay out here *furlong*."

Word: furlough

True definition: leave of absence

Smittionary
"Not your ordinary dictionary"
To get the best effect, say the italicized word(s) slowly

My definition: animal protective covering

Sentence: "In the summer months, they try to keep the bears *furlough* so they don't overheat!"

Word: fussy

True definition: an action of anger

My definition: a look to the future

Sentence: "Anything could happen, but I don't *fussy* any problems!"

Smittionary
"Not your ordinary dictionary"
To get the best effect, say the italicized word(s) slowly

G

Word: Galileo
True definition: a physicist
My definition: a female's zodiac sign
Sentence: "Awww, she's lying. She ain't no Capricorn! That *Galileo!*"

Word: Galloway
True definition: a breed of Scottish beef cattle
My definition: sending someone on a trip
Sentence: "He is so nice because he sent his *Galloway* on a cruise!"

Word: gamma
True definition: the third letter of the Greek alphabet
My definition: your mother's or father's mother
Sentence: "Are we going to *Gamma* and Gampa's house?"

Smittionary
"Not your ordinary dictionary"
To get the best effect, say the italicized word(s) slowly

Word: gangrene

True definition: death of tissue because of lack of blood supply

My definition: an amateur crime group

Sentence: "They tried to do a drive-by with water pistols! That *gangrene* behind the ears!"

Word: gasometer

True definition: a gas measuring device

My definition: being stood up

Sentence: "My blind date didn't show up at the restaurant. I *gasometer* later!"

Word: Gatineau

True definition: the name of a river in Canada

My definition: familiarizing yourself with someone

Sentence: "They are not bad people once you *Gatineau* them!"

Word: gaucho

True definition: a cowboy of the South American pampas

My definition: something obtained

Sentence: "We 'bout to go in the party. You *gaucho* ID ready?"

Smittionary
"Not your ordinary dictionary"
To get the best effect, say the italicized word(s) slowly

Word: gee whiz

True definition: expression designed to arouse wonder or excitement

My definition: a person who knows everything about gangsters

Sentence: "Man, he is like a gangsta dictionary. He's a *gee whiz*!"

Word: geminate

True definition: to arrange in pairs

My definition: alternate place to eat

Sentence: "The school cafeteria was closed, so all the kids went into the *geminate* their lunches."

Word: Gemini

True definition: a zodiac sign

My definition: when you include your husband Jim in a decision

Sentence: "The offer looks great, but *Gemini* have decided to wait awhile."

Word: genealogy

True definition: study of family descendants

My definition: when your eyes run and you sneeze around genies

43

Smittionary
"Not your ordinary dictionary"
To get the best effect, say the italicized word(s) slowly

Sentence: "He really started sneezing bad after he rubbed the bottle. He must have a *genealogy*!"

Word: generalize
True definition: to commonly group together
My definition: a high-ranking military official who doesn't tell the truth
Sentence: "Looks like the *generalize* to the troops again about deployment!"

Word: generate
True definition: to bring into existence
My definition: a famous former athlete's appetite
Sentence: "He must have been starving because Mr. *generate* all the meatballs and potato salad!"

Word: genuine
True definition: sincere or honest
My definition: drunk from gin
Sentence: "I tried to drink more, but I am toasted. Okay, *genuine* this time!"

Word: geometry
True definition: a form of mathematics

Smittionary
"Not your ordinary dictionary"
To get the best effect, say the italicized word(s) slowly

My definition: something a baby tree would say

Sentence: "As it looked at its branches, the maple said, '*geometry*!'"

Word: geyser

True definition: a spring that emits steamed water

My definition: a group of males

Sentence: "We have with us a bunch of comedians because these *geyser* crazy!"

Word: ghosting

True definition: a double image on a television screen

My definition: directing a bee or wasp

Sentence: "Okay, I see you swarming, and I am not in the mood. So *ghosting* somebody else!"

Word: giddyap

True definition: a command to a horse while riding

My definition: obtaining a new iPhone application

Sentence: "That new game looks fun. I will *giddyap* downloaded tomorrow!"

Smittionary
"Not your ordinary dictionary"
To get the best effect, say the italicized word(s) slowly

Word: gigabytes

True definition: one billion bytes

My definition: what my dog named Giga does

Sentence: "Don't tease my dog. If *Gigabytes* you, it's your own fault!"

Word: gigahertz

True definition: one billion hertz of frequency

My definition: the result if "Gigabytes"

Sentence: "If 'Gigabytes' you, then *Gigahertz* you!"

Word: gigabit

True definition: one billion bits of information

My definition: what "Giga" did

Sentence: "*Gigabit* me once…and only once!"

Word: gigawatt

True definition: one billion watts of power as in a radio station's power

My definition: spoiling your dog

Sentence: "Since he is so mean, I give *Gigawatt* ever he wants!"

Smittionary
"Not your ordinary dictionary"
To get the best effect, say the italicized word(s) slowly

Word: gigaflop

True definition: unit of measuring the speed of a computer

My definition: what Giga did after "Gigabit" me

Sentence: "I smacked Giga with a rolled-up newspaper, and *gigaflop* on the ground!"

Word: Gillette

True definition: a company that makes razors and shaving cream

My definition: something allowed

Sentence: "Why *Gillette* them go in the first place?"

Word: gin rummy

True definition: a card game

My definition: results of drinking

Sentence: "I hate to complain, but that *gin rummy* to the bathroom a lot!"

Word: giraffe

True definition: a spotted animal with a long neck

My definition: a small boat made from logs

Sentence: "Did *giraffe* sink when it had a hole in it?"

Smittionary
"Not your ordinary dictionary"
To get the best effect, say the italicized word(s) slowly

Word: gizmo
True definition: a gadget
My definition: receives
Sentence: "He *gizmo* attention after he shaved his beard off!"

Word: gladiator
True definition: a Roman soldier
My definition: food consumption
Sentence: "She's so *gladiator* food she cooked!"

Word: glaucoma
True definition: a disease of the eyes
My definition: a type of gun
Sentence: "The police officer said, 'I think I left my *glaucoma* dresser!'"

Word: gloomy
True definition: dark, depressing
My definition: attach with adhesive
Sentence: "I had fun helping with the kids crafts until they tried to *gloomy* to the floor!"

Word: glossator
True definition: one who compiles a glossary
My definition: ladies' lip product

Smittionary
"Not your ordinary dictionary"
To get the best effect, say the italicized word(s) slowly

Sentence: "She regrets switching makeup brands because that new lip *glossator* skin off her lips!"

Word: Goliath

True definition: a Philistine killed by David in the Bible

My definition: to rest on your back, side, or stomach

Sentence: "Her kid was in a terrible mood, so she told him to *Goliath* down for a few minutes!"

Word: Gomez

True definition: name of a Venezuelan dictator

My definition: suggesting someone bother other people

Sentence: "I am not in the mood today, so *Gomez* with somebody else!"

Word: goodwill

True definition: a kindly feeling of approval or support

My definition: a defect-free car tire

Sentence: "This car has one *goodwill* and three bad ones!"

Smittionary
"Not your ordinary dictionary"
To get the best effect, say the italicized word(s) slowly

Word: gopher

True definition: a rodent that burrows in the ground

My definition: hunger request

Sentence: "I'm so hungry that I could *gopher* a thick juicy cheeseburger!"

Word: gruesome

True definition: gory or morbidly scary

My definition: what happens after you plant something

Sentence: "In my new garden, I *gruesome* tomatoes, turnips, and green beans!"

Word: guesstimate

True definition: estimate made without adequate information

My definition: hosting an event

Sentence: "I don't have time for foolishness because I've got important *guesstimate*!"

Word: guidance

True definition: someone offering direction

My definition: a male partying move

Sentence: "She said, 'I can't move like that because that's a *guidance*!'"

Smittionary
"Not your ordinary dictionary"
To get the best effect, say the italicized word(s) slowly

Word: guitar

True definition: a musical instrument with strings

My definition: wheel on a car or truck

Sentence: "With all that tread, that is definitely a *guitar* on the left front!"

Smittionary
"Not your ordinary dictionary"
To get the best effect, say the italicized word(s) slowly

H

Word: habilitate

True definition: to make fit or capable

My definition: making Billy the guinea pig for your cooking

Sentence: "I'm scared to eat this new dish I made, so I'll *habilitate* it first to see if he likes it!"

Word: hammertoe

True definition: a deformed claw-shaped toe

My definition: an amateur with a tool

Sentence: "Take that tool away from him now! He and that *hammertoe* up more than they fixed!"

Word: hamper

True definition: to curb or restrain or a dirty clothes' storage bin

My definition: restrictions on famous hams

Smittionary
"Not your ordinary dictionary"
To get the best effect, say the italicized word(s) slowly

Sentence: "Just so we don't run out, we have only allowed one *hamper* family!"

Word: handsome
True definition: an attractive male
My definition: giving of an item
Sentence: "I don't know what he was thinking because I just saw him *handsome* girl his wallet!"

Word: handyman
True definition: one who does odd jobs
My definition: teaching a young one how to buy something
Sentence: "Go ahead and *handyman* your money so he can ring you up!"

Word: harem
True definition: a group of women belonging to one man
My definition: listening to something
Sentence: "I just moved in, and the new neighbors are so loud you can *harem* a mile away!"

Word: Havana
True definition: a Cuban cigar

Smittionary
"Not your ordinary dictionary"
To get the best effect, say the italicized word(s) slowly

My definition: a lady that assists on a popular letter game show

Sentence: "Okay, Pat, can you *Havana* turn another letter, please?"

Word: haymaker

True definition: a powerful blow

My definition: forcing someone to do something

Sentence: "She was not happy when *haymaker* quit her job yesterday!"

Word: haywire

True definition: chaos or out of order

My definition: asking someone their destination

Sentence: "*Haywire* y'all going for vacation?"

Word: hazmat

True definition: short for hazardous materials

My definition: someone who was introduced to someone

Sentence: "I'm sure he *hazmat* my cousin already!"

Word: header

True definition: a brick or stone laid facing a wall

Smittionary
"Not your ordinary dictionary"
To get the best effect, say the italicized word(s) slowly

My definition: action against someone

Sentence: "She hit him with a brick so he *header* arrested!"

Word: Hebrews

True definition: a book of the Bible

My definition: what you do with coffee or tea

Sentence: "He should work for Starbucks because *Hebrews* the best coffee I ever tasted!"

Word: heifer

True definition: a young cow

My definition: directing someone to do something

Sentence: "When she gets back home, can you *heifer* to call me?"

Word: hepatitis

True definition: inflammation of the liver

My definition: assisting a woman in tying rope

Sentence: "Who's gonna *hepatitis* rope around the tree to make a swing?"

Word: hepatoma

True definition: tumor of the liver

Smittionary
"Not your ordinary dictionary"
To get the best effect, say the italicized word(s) slowly

My definition: help with car trouble

Sentence: "The tow-truck driver *hepatoma* car to the shop when it wouldn't start!"

Word: hermit

True definition: one who lives in solitude

My definition: a female's softball glove

Sentence: "I can't put her in the game because she left *hermit* at home!"

Word: hero

True definition: a person admired for his strength and accomplishments

My definition: what a man does with oars

Sentence: "I knew he was going to win the race 'cause *hero* that kayak like a champ!"

Word: Hertz

True definition: a car rental company

My definition: pain

Sentence: "I stumped my toe, and it really *Hertz* a lot!"

Word: hifalutin

True definition: pretentious or fancy

My definition: a flute player on drugs

Smittionary
"Not your ordinary dictionary"
To get the best effect, say the italicized word(s) slowly

Sentence: "The band sounded good except for that *hifalutin* girl! She smelled like marijuana was out of tune bad!"

Word: highjack
True definition: attempt to take over a plane or other mode of transportation
My definition: speaking to your friend named Jack
Sentence: "Well, *highjack*. How have you been?"

Word: Hindu
True definition: a native of India
My definition: a farm animal's actions
Sentence: "I agree that *Hindu* lay more eggs than the chickens!"

Word: honey
True definition: something bees help produce
My definition: a female leg part
Sentence: "Little Susie is crying because she fell and scraped *honey*!"

Word: honeycomb
True definition: waxy cells built by bees

Smittionary
"Not your ordinary dictionary"
To get the best effect, say the italicized word(s) slowly

My definition: encouraging your daughter to fix her hair

Sentence: "We are going out shopping, so *honeycomb* your hair!"

Word: honeydew

True definition: a type of melon

My definition: what your spouse asks of you

Sentence: "It's always *honeydew* this and *honeydew* that around my household!"

Word: honor

True definition: praise or a good name

My definition: something on a female

Sentence: "She's dressed really nice except for that stain *honor* blouse!"

Word(s): honor roll

True definition: a list of students with academic distinction

My definition: something on your food

Sentence: "I think she has lost her appetite because she saw a fly *honor roll*."

Word: hoodoo

True definition: to cast a spell on or to bring bad luck to

Smittionary
"Not your ordinary dictionary"
To get the best effect, say the italicized word(s) slowly

My definition: someone's profession

Sentence: "Does anybody know anyone *hoo-doo* tinted windows?"

Word: hoodwink

True definition: to deceive

My definition: a physical gesture with the eyes

Sentence: "We sat and watched that *hoodwink* at every woman that walked by!"

Word: Hoosier

True definition: a native of Indiana

My definition: asking someone a personal question

Sentence: "I know I'm meddling, but *Hoosier* sister dating now?"

Word: hosanna

True definition: a cry of declaration or adoration

My definition: a watering device

Sentence: "To water your lawn, all you need is a water *hosanna* nozzle!"

Word: hospital

True definition: health-care facility

Smittionary
"Not your ordinary dictionary"
To get the best effect, say the italicized word(s) slowly

My definition: a Western TV character's bad habit

Sentence: "That was nasty when *hospital* his chewing tobacco juice on Little Joe's boot!"

Word: huffy

True definition: easily offended

My definition: dues

Sentence: "She got arrested for not paying *huffy* for the speeding ticket!"

Word: hunger

True definition: craving for food

My definition: what the woman did with her stockings

Sentence: "After she washed clothes, she *hunger* pantyhose in the bathroom to dry!"

Smittionary
"Not your ordinary dictionary"
To get the best effect, say the italicized word(s) slowly

I

Word: Idaho
True definition: one of the fifty
    states
My definition: a conceited woman
Sentence: "She said, 'I got beauty,
    brains, and money! *Idaho*
    package!'"

Word: illegal
True definition: against the law
My definition: a sick bird
Sentence: "Here at the animal hospital, we
    have two ill ducks, four ill cats, one ill
    snake, and one *illegal*."

Word: illiterate
True definition: not able to read
My definition: a small sick rodent
Sentence: "I feel sorry for him because he sure
    is an *illiterate*!"

Smittionary
"Not your ordinary dictionary"
To get the best effect, say the italicized word(s) slowly

Word: immensity
True definition: the condition of greatness
My definition: stuck in traffic
Sentence: "I drove to New York and *immensity* traffic, and it's bumper-to-bumper!"

Word: impairs
True definition: makes worse
My definition: fruit
Sentence: "She liked the apples, but *impairs* were delicious!"

Word: impatience
True definition: not willing to wait for something or intolerance
My definition: those hospital residents
Sentence: "I know they are sick, but *impatience* are beginning to get on my nerves!"

Word: impeaches
True definition: the act of removing an official from office
My definition: fruit
Sentence: "'Impairs' were good, but *impeaches* tasted a lot better!"

Smittionary
"Not your ordinary dictionary"
To get the best effect, say the italicized word(s) slowly

Word: imposed

True definition: to force your presence on someone

My definition: standing for a picture

Sentence: "When the photographer told him to smile, *imposed* for the camera like a pro!"

Word: identifier

True definition: one who recognizes something

My definition: a wreck with an emergency vehicle

Sentence: "I didn't hear any sirens. And next thing I know, I couldn't stop, and I think *identifier* truck!"

Word: idolize

True meaning: to worship something or someone

My definition: when your friend named Ida doesn't tell the truth

Sentence: "Y'all can believe her if you want to, but *idolize* all the time!"

Word: immature

True definition: childish acting

Smittionary
"Not your ordinary dictionary"
To get the best effect, say the italicized word(s) slowly

My definition: when your baby named Emma
   learns how to eat correctly

Sentence: "I am so proud of my baby! *Immature*
   food really good before swallowing!"

Word: immense

True definition: marked by greatness

My definition: breath fresheners

Sentence: "I just ate some onions! Can you
   hand me some of *immense*?"

Word: immigrate

True definition: to settle into another country

My definition: a compliment

Sentence: "I don't usually eat meatballs someone else cooked, but *immigrate*!"

Word: incipit

True definition: the first words of a text

My definition: drinking etiquette

Sentence: "Don't pour your brandy and gulp
   it! Pour it over ice *incipit*!"

Word: incite

True definition: to put into motion

My definition: locating something

Sentence: "I have located the ship, and I now
   have them *incite*!"

Smittionary
"Not your ordinary dictionary"
To get the best effect, say the italicized word(s) slowly

Word: incomparable

True definition: something that cannot be matched or compared with

My definition: a clever story about your earnings

Sentence: "To help you understand your finances, I wrote an *incomparable* for you!"

Word: indecency

True definition: inappropriate or not presentable

My definition: If the state of Indiana and the city of Cincinnati merged, this will be the name!

Sentence: "Since Indiana is close to Cincinnati, I'll just call that middle area *indecency*."

Word: indecent

True definition: not presentable or offensive

My definition: surrounded by a smell

Sentence: "Someone passed gas, and I walked right *indecent*!"

Word: independent

True definition: not relying on others

My definition: a piece of jewelry representing the state of Indiana

Smittionary
"Not your ordinary dictionary"
To get the best effect, say the italicized word(s) slowly

Sentence: "She loves Indiana because she wears her *independent* around her neck every day!"

Word: index
True definition: a reference point for a book
My definition: construction terminology
Sentence: "Building porches is okay, but there's more money to be made *index* added to houses!"

Word: Indianapolis
True definition: city in the state of Indiana
My definition: law enforcers on the reservation whose only job is to arrest people for sleeping
Sentence: "Chief Bighorn got arrested again for taking a nap by the *Indianapolis*."

Word: indiscreet
True definition: not showing good judgement with actions
My definition: where kids play sometimes
Sentence: "Tell Mimi her kids are playing *indiscreet* again and gonna get hit by a car!"

Smittionary
"Not your ordinary dictionary"
To get the best effect, say the italicized word(s) slowly

Word: indispose

True definition: to make unfit

My definition: modeling moves

Sentence: "Looking at your photo shoot, I really like you *indispose* better!"

Word: indium

True definition: a metallic substance used in electronics

My definition: a trait you are born with

Sentence: "I know for a fact that them kids have a little craziness *indium*."

Word: Indochina

True definition: a country

My definition: dishes not to be used outside

Sentence: "Oh, please, don't take those plates outside because that's my *Indochina*!"

Word: indwell

True definition: to exist as an inner spirit or position

My definition: the last part of a cliché

Sentence: "All's well that *indwell*!"

Smittionary
"Not your ordinary dictionary"
To get the best effect, say the italicized word(s) slowly

Word: inertia

True definition: something that remains in a
    rest condition

My definition: an assistant at church

Sentence: "It was so crowded at the church
    that *inertia* had to help me find a seat!"

Word: infamy

True definition: a public criminal or evil act

My definition: someone plotting against you

Sentence: "I don't know what I did, but some-
    one has it *infamy*!"

Word: inferno

True definition: an intense fire

My definition: wrongfully arrested

Sentence: "I am innocent. That cop took me
    inferno reason at all!"

Word: infest

True definition: to swarm or live inside
    something

My definition: quick action

Sentence: "I wish they would slow this bus
    down! It's like we're going *infest* motion!"

Smittionary
"Not your ordinary dictionary"
To get the best effect, say the italicized word(s) slowly

Word: infidel
True definition: an unbeliever in something
My definition: a country's leader
Sentence: "When you are in Cuba, you are *infidel* Castro's country!"

Word: inglorious
True definition: lacking honor of fame
My definition: a lady's name
Sentence: "Just put the packages *inglorious* trunk!"

Word: inhale
True definition: to breathe in
My definition: where Satan resides
Sentence: "If you keep doing bad things, you can wind up *inhale*!"

Word: inoculate
True definition: to insert an organism into something for growth
My definition: a tardy Bible character
Sentence: "I can't believe it! *Inoculate* again for the tent meeting again!"

Word: inquire
True definition: to ask about

Smittionary
"Not your ordinary dictionary"
To get the best effect, say the italicized word(s) slowly

My definition: a singing group

Sentence: "Bob got in trouble for acting up *inquire* practice last night."

Word: insinuate

True definition: to suggest in an indirect way

My definition: eating chicken wings at a strip club

Sentence: "*Insinuate* those wings, so repent!"

Word: instantiate

True definition: to represent by a concrete instance

My definition: the result of eating too much

Sentence: "She got full the *instantiate* the appetizer!"

Word: instantly

True definition: urgently or right now

My definition: ladies' finger accessories

Sentence: "Fixing my nails were so easy since I bought those *instantly* nails!"

Word: insulate

True definition: to pack with material to keep warm or cold

My definition: coming in after-hours

Smittionary
"Not your ordinary dictionary"
To get the best effect, say the italicized word(s) slowly

Sentence: "Last night, I got *insulate* that I heard the roosters crowing!"

Word: integrated
True definition: coming together collectively
My definition: cheese preparation
Sentence: "Some people are into sliced cheese, but I am *integrated* cheese myself!"

Word: intense
True definition: an extreme degree
My definition: camping housing
Sentence: "The Boy Scouts usually sleep *intense* when camping."

Word: intensifier
True definition: something that makes things excessive
My definition: a nonrecommended flame
Sentence: "When camping, *intensifier* is not allowed inside because it may burn to the ground!"

Word: interim
True definition: to substitute temporarily

Smittionary
"Not your ordinary dictionary"
To get the best effect, say the italicized word(s) slowly

My definition: to sign your son up for an event

Sentence: "My boy spells so good I think I'll *interim* in the next spelling bee!"

Word: interiorize
True definition: to process or do a task inside
My definition: gazing
Sentence: "When I look *interiorize*, I can see your pupils!"

Word: interrogated
True definition: questioned repeatedly
My definition: going through a private fenced community
Sentence: "The next time I *interrogated* subdivision, I'll drive a little slower!"

Word: interrogator
True definition: one who questions repeatedly
My definition: a woman avoiding damaging her footwear
Sentence: "She didn't like walking through the rocks because she didn't want to fall *interrogator* boots up!"

Smittionary
"Not your ordinary dictionary"
To get the best effect, say the italicized word(s) slowly

Word: ion
True definition: a charged particle in the air
My definition: watching someone closely
Sentence: "You'd best behave because I got my *ion* you!"

Word: Iowa
True definition: one of the fifty states
My definition: debt
Sentence: "I went crazy for Christmas, and now *Iowa* lot of money to credit cards!"

Word: Ishmael
True definition: son of Abraham and Hagar
My definition: stinky
Sentence: "I don't mean to complain, but *Ishmael* like garbage in here!"

Word: isolate
True definition: to set apart
My definition: tardiness
Sentence: "I tried to be on time, but *isolate* for my meeting I think I'll skip it!"

Word: isometry
True definition: a mapping of a metric space onto another or onto itself with equal distances

Smittionary
"Not your ordinary dictionary"
To get the best effect, say the italicized word(s) slowly

My definition: witnessing the effects of a storm

Sentence: "The wind was blowing so hard that *isometry* bend to the ground then upright itself!"

Word: Israelite

True definition: a descendant or Israel

My definition: the weight of something

Sentence: "This bag *Israelite*, so I can carry it myself!"

Smittionary
"Not your ordinary dictionary"
To get the best effect, say the italicized word(s) slowly

J

Word: jabberwocky

True definition: meaningless speech

My definition: a famous movie boxer

Sentence: "That right-hand *jabberwocky* won another fight in the movie!"

Word: jacket

True definition: outerwear

My definition: what you do to your car

Sentence: "To change a tire on your car, you have to *jacket* up first!"

Word: jackhammer

True definition: a tool used to break up concrete

My definition: allowing someone else to help in construction work

Sentence: "Okay, guys, we will let *jackhammer* in the last nail!"

Smittionary
"Not your ordinary dictionary"
To get the best effect, say the italicized word(s) slowly

Word: jailbait

True definition: a girl under the age of consent

My definition: what prisoners go fishing with…and one reason some of them are in prison!

Sentence: "One prisoner raised a worm farm in his cell so he could fish with *jailbait*."

Word: Jamaica

True definition: an island for tourism

My definition: something you did

Sentence: "How did *Jamaica* mess that quick?"

Word: jasmine

True definition: a plant with fragrant flowers or a yellowish color

My definition: music legends

Sentence: "Duke Ellington was one of the many great *jasmine* of our time!"

Word: jaundice

True definition: a yellowish pigmentation of the skin

My definition: giving John direction

Sentence: "Hey, *jaundice* box needs to go over there with the other ones!"

Smittionary
"Not your ordinary dictionary"
To get the best effect, say the italicized word(s) slowly

Word: jealous

True definition: envious toward someone

My definition: to imprison

Sentence: "We were innocent, but the cops still tried to arrest and *jealous* with no charges!"

Word: jester

True definition: another name for a fool in medieval days

My definition: country slang for the phrase "just a"

Sentence: "Now hold on *jester* minute!"

Smittionary
"Not your ordinary dictionary"
To get the best effect, say the italicized word(s) slowly

K

Word: keloids

True definition: scars resulting from growth of fibrous tissue

My definition: scratching Lloyd's vehicle

Sentence: "We got outside just in time because somebody tried to *keloids* truck!"

Word: ketchup

True definition: a condiment made with tomatoes

My definition: a word used when someone leaves you

Sentence: "Hey, wait, let me *ketchup* with you!"

Word: kidnapping

True definition: to take a person for a ransom

My definition: a sleeping child

Smittionary
"Not your ordinary dictionary"
To get the best effect, say the italicized word(s) slowly

Sentence: "I have to go wake little Jimmy up because I don't want my *kidnapping* all day!"

Word: kidneys
True definition: a pair of organs in the body
My definition: a child's bendable leg part
Sentence: "Her legs were so skinny it looked like she had a pair of *kidneys*!"

Word: Kongo
True definition: a member of the Bantu people near the Congo River
My definition: giving permission
Sentence: "I may regret this later, but you *Kongo* to the party!"

Smittionary
"Not your ordinary dictionary"
To get the best effect, say the italicized word(s) slowly

L

Word: lacquer

True definition: a wax sealer

My definition: fond of someone

Sentence: "She's cute and nice, and I really *lacquer* a lot!"

Word: ladies

True definition: another word for women

My definition: the placing of items

Sentence: "Hey, can you *ladies* papers on my desk, please?"

Word: ladybug

True definition: a spotted bug from beetle family

My definition: instructing your child to dispose of a dead bug

Sentence: "Charlie! The cricket is dead, so please *ladybug* on the ground!"

Smittionary
"Not your ordinary dictionary"
To get the best effect, say the italicized word(s) slowly

Word: landfill

True definition: a place where garbage and waste is dumped

My definition: Phillip the pilot getting clearance from the airport tower

Sentence: "This is tower control. You are clear to *landfill*."

Word: Lassie

True definition: a young girl or a famous TV dog

My definition: checking out a situation

Sentence: "So your cable went out? *Lassie* what's going on with your signal!"

Word: laughter

True definition: the result of something funny

My definition: leaving someone

Sentence: "She didn't want to go to the game, so he *laughter* at home!"

Word: lava

True definition: molten rock from a volcano

My definition: Don Juan-like

Sentence: "She called me her *lava* boy!"

Smittionary
"Not your ordinary dictionary"
To get the best effect, say the italicized word(s) slowly

Word: lawbreaker

True definition: someone who violates the law

My definition: what the cops did to the woman

Sentence: "She sued the entire police department claiming the *lawbreaker* arm in two places!"

Word: lawgiver

True definition: one who gives a code of law to a person

My definition: cop choices

Sentence: "The *lawgiver* two choices: to drop the weapon or get shot!"

Word: layette

True definition: complete equipment and clothing for a newborn baby

My definition: setting something down or installing

Sentence: "I got some new carpet, and I'll try to *layette* myself!"

Word: layover

True definition: the time between planes at the airport

My definition: a Hawaiian tradition

Smittionary
"Not your ordinary dictionary"
To get the best effect, say the italicized word(s) slowly

Sentence: "When I arrived in Hawaii, a pretty lady put a *layover* my head and around my neck!"

Word: leaven
True definition: a substance like yeast used in bread
My definition: a number
Sentence: "Eight, nine, ten…*leaven*."

Word: legacy
True definition: something left by an ancestor
My definition: body part
Sentence: "When you lift your *legacy* your calf muscles!"

Word: leisure
True definition: relaxation or downtime
My definition: having a cousin named Lee
Sentence: "I think I have met all your family, so *leisure* first cousin, right?"

Word: Lent
True definition: fasting season during Easter
My definition: a loan
Sentence: "I *Lent* him ten dollars last week, and he ain't paid me back yet!"

Smittionary
"Not your ordinary dictionary"
To get the best effect, say the italicized word(s) slowly

Word: Lenten

True definition: Easter tradition season

My definition: another loan

Sentence: "He hadn't paid back the last ten dollars when he asked me to *Lenten* more to him!"

Word: lessee

True definition: one who holds property under a lease

My definition: checking out an issue

Sentence: "So you say your car won't start? *Lessee* what the problem is!"

Word: letter

True definition: a symbol or note that is written or typed

My definition: allowing

Sentence: "Why did you just *letter* hit you in the eye?"

Word: lettuce

True definition: a leafy vegetable used in salad

My definition: to allow

Sentence: "Hey, Jimmy. Go see if mom will *lettuce* go outside!"

Smittionary
"Not your ordinary dictionary"
To get the best effect, say the italicized word(s) slowly

Word: leukemogenesis

True definition: induction or production of leukemia

My definition: showing off your new Hyundai luxury car

Sentence: "Hey, y'all! *Leukemogenesis*! I just bought it!"

Word: leukemia

True definition: a disease that causes an increase in white blood cells

My definition: calling your friend Lou over for something

Sentence: "Hey, *leukemia*. I want to show you something!"

Word: leukotomy

True definition: same as lobotomy

My definition: my friend Lou turning me in

Sentence: "I went to the store, and *leukotomy* stealing again!"

Word: licentiate

True definition: a person who is granted a license by a university, etc. to perform a practice

Smittionary
"Not your ordinary dictionary"
To get the best effect, say the italicized word(s) slowly

My definition: blaming a fibbing habit on food

Sentence: "I don't know what was in that chili, but she started to *licentiate* it!"

Word: lilac

True definition: a flower or a shade of purple

My definition: someone who doesn't tell the truth

Sentence: "Don't trust him 'cause he *lilac* this all the time!"

Word: limeade

True definition: a drink made with sweetened lime juice and water

My definition: untruthful discovery

Sentence: "She was under oath, but that last *limeade* the jury suspicious!"

Word: lionize

True definition: to treat as a person of great interest

My definition: a look when someone doesn't tell the truth

Sentence: "He's not telling the truth because he's got those *lionize*!"

Smittionary
"Not your ordinary dictionary"
To get the best effect, say the italicized word(s) slowly

Word: lipoprotein

True definition: complex solution of protein and lipid

My definition: a person who has had many liposuction surgeries between the ages of thirteen and nineteen

Sentence: "She has had so many fat-reducing surgeries I think I'll call her a *lipoprotein*!"

Word: lipstick

True definition: makeup for the lips

My definition: an embarrassing situation

Sentence: "They told Hank to put his mouth on the frozen pole just to see his *lipstick* to it!"

Word: liquor

True definition: alcoholic beverage

My definition: a tasting maneuver

Sentence: "He got popped in the eye because he tried to *liquor* ice-cream cone!"

Word: literacy

True definition: the quality or state of being literate

My definition: commenting on your friend's cat's babies

Smittionary
"Not your ordinary dictionary"
To get the best effect, say the italicized word(s) slowly

Sentence: "Wow! I counted ten baby kittens. Your cat had a nice *literacy*!"

Word: literate
True definition: able to read and write
My definition: trashing something
Sentence: "Hey! Look at mean Mr. Jones's nice yard. Let's *literate* with trash and toilet paper!"

Word: lithium
True definition: additive to batteries to prolong life
My definition: adding fire to something
Sentence: "There were one hundred candles on his birthday cake, and they *lithium* all!"

Word: litigator
True definition: one who carries on a legal process
My definition: a cruel animal act
Sentence: "The boys were arrested for animal cruelty because they *litigator* on fire in the swamp!"

Smittionary
"Not your ordinary dictionary"
To get the best effect, say the italicized word(s) slowly

Word: livid
True definition: very angry
My definition: a choice
Sentence: "Life. You either choose to *livid* or
you don't!"

Word: loafer
True definition: a low step-in shoe
My definition: a great deal
Sentence: "These shirts must be on sale because
the price is awful *loafer* this store!"

Word: lo mein
True definition: a Chinese food dish
My definition: no seniority
Sentence: "I'm a new employee here, so I'm
the *lo mein* on the totem pole!"

Word: lotus
True definition: a variety of water lilies
My definition: a crowd entering something
Sentence: "I can't believe they wanted to *lotus*
all in that little bitty bus!"

Word: lovable
True definition: having qualities to be very
well-liked

Smittionary
"Not your ordinary dictionary"
To get the best effect, say the italicized word(s) slowly

My definition: a food request

Sentence: "Hey, waitress. I'd really *lovable* of soup with my meal, please!"

Word: luau

True definition: a Hawaiian feast and festival

My definition: a former pro basketball player

Sentence: "Before he changed his name, Kareem Abdul Jabbar's real name was *Luau* Cinder!"

Word: Lew Alcindor

True definition: Kareem Abdul Jabbar's birth name

My definition: your boss Lou's request to see a female employee

Sentence: "You need to see Margaret? Okay, *Lew Alcindor* in immediately!"

Word: lucent

True definition: glowing with light

My definition: adjourned meeting

Sentence: "Just as requested, *lucent* Margaret to see the boss!"

Word: Lucifer

True definition: the devil

Smittionary
"Not your ordinary dictionary"
To get the best effect, say the italicized word(s) slowly

My definition: a surprise

Sentence: "Ricky, with a new car, surprised *Lucifer* her birthday!"

Word: ludicrous

True definition: amusing or laughable through obvious absurdity or exaggeration

My definition: a warning to Lou about baked goods

Sentence: "Leave my pie in the oven, *ludicrous* isn't done yet!"

Word: lugger

True definition: a small fishing boat

My definition: dragging someone

Sentence: "After she collapsed, he had to *lugger* from the sidewalk to the porch!"

Word: lukewarm

True definition: a mild temperature

My definition: new-shoes appreciation

Sentence: "After I bought him the new Jordans, *lukewarm* every day!"

Word: Lutheran

True definition: religious doctrine

My definition: a marathon runner

Smittionary
"Not your ordinary dictionary"
To get the best effect, say the italicized word(s) slowly

Sentence: "For the world's record, *Lutheran* the mile in under two minutes!"

Word: luxuriance
True definition: the state of yielding abundantly
My definition: your father's rich sisters
Sentence: "My father's two sisters have a boat-load of money, so I always call them my *luxuriance*!"

Word: luxuriate
True definition: to grow profusely
My definition: trying a new delicacy
Sentence: "I, knowing I was surrounded by *luxuriate* some escargot and caviar!"

Word: lymphadenitis
True definition: inflammation of the lymph nodes
My definition: faking a leg injury
Sentence: "He always fakes a leg injury! I can't wait to see what his *lymphadenitis*!"

Word: Lipitor
True definition: medicine used to lower lipid levels in the blood
My definition: mouth injury

Smittionary
"Not your ordinary dictionary"
To get the best effect, say the italicized word(s) slowly

Sentence: "She hit her so hard in the *Lipitor* off some of the skin!"

Word: lymphoma
True definition: lymphoid tissue tumor
My definition: a stuttered walking condition
Sentence: "Yes, my leg hurts! Do you think I *lymphoma* health?"

Word: lymphomatosis
True definition: the presence of lymph nodes in the body
My definition: explaining to your sister why you walk funny
Sentence: "You asked me why, so I'll tell ya. You see, I *lymphomatosis*, the big one 'cause it is broken!"

Smittionary
"Not your ordinary dictionary"
To get the best effect, say the italicized word(s) slowly

M

Word: Macao

True definition: a peninsula of China

My definition: livestock

Sentence: "Call the veterinarian! *Macao* stopped giving milk all of a sudden!"

Word: machine

True definition: something made with parts to do a task

My definition: glossiness

Sentence: "I Just cleaned my car! Look at *machine* on that wax job!"

Word: machismo

True definition: a true sense of masculine pride

My definition: unmelted dairy product

Sentence: "My macaroni was okay, but I should have melted *machismo*!"

Smittionary
"Not your ordinary dictionary"
To get the best effect, say the italicized word(s) slowly

Word: mafia
True definition: an organized crime family
My definition: overcoming a phobia
Sentence: "I really have to get over *mafia* of flying!"

Word: magazine
True definition: a book containing stories, pictures, and ads
My definition: drawing unneeded attention
Sentence: "I know you don't like them, but just don't do anything to *magazine*!"

Word: magenta
True definition: a deep purplish-red color
My definition: chivalry
Sentence: "Yes, I still hold the door open for women because I *magenta* man!"

Word: maggot
True definition: a white larvae-type bug usually found in decomposing bodies or trash
My definition: a strong feeling within
Sentence: "I'm gonna go with *maggot* feeling and not buy this car because the deal looks shady!"

Smittionary
"Not your ordinary dictionary"
To get the best effect, say the italicized word(s) slowly

Word: magna cum laude

True definition: graduation with distinction or high honor

My definition: a gospel song

Sentence: "For our first selection, we will be singing '*magna cum laude*!'"

Word: magnolia

True definition: a type of tree

My definition: questioning Meg's friends

Sentence: "I've never seen you around here before! Where does *magnolia* from?"

Word: maiden

True definition: an unmarried girl or woman

My definition: where an item is produced

Sentence: "See, I told ya it is not from here! It says right on the label, *maiden* China!"

Word: mainstay

True definition: a part of a ship

My definition: helping a friend through a breakup

Sentence: "You really couldn't make that *main-stay* if you wanted to!"

Smittionary
"Not your ordinary dictionary"
To get the best effect, say the italicized word(s) slowly

Word: majorette

True definition: a female accompanying a band that twirls a baton or flag

My definition: a big rodent

Sentence: "Man! That is one *majorette* you caught in that trap!"

Word: maladjustment

True definition: a poor or bad tweak of something

My definition: illegal odometer turn-back for less miles on a car

Sentence: "He got arrested for doing a *maladjustment* on his car before selling it!"

Word: Manchu

True definition: settlers in China and a language

My definition: eating

Sentence: "Since he got his new dentures, that *Manchu* his steak very carefully!"

Word: mandate

True definition: an official order

My definition: a player

Sentence: "He's a true player! That *mandate* a different girl every week!"

Smittionary
"Not your ordinary dictionary"
To get the best effect, say the italicized word(s) slowly

Word: mannered

True definition: well-behaved

My definition: your geeky sibling

Sentence: "So you said your computer locked up? I bet *mannered* brother can fix it!"

Word: mantic

True definition: relating to divination or to be prophetic

My definition: making someone mad or upset

Sentence: "Girl, there's Charles! Please don't let that *mantic* you off again this week!"

Word: manure

True definition: animal waste used as fertilizer

My definition: denying you know someone

Sentence: "He said he had never seen her before, but I'm sure that *manure* from somewhere!"

Word: many

True definition: a large number

My definition: bendable leg part

Sentence: "Go get me a Band-Aid. I just fell and scraped *many*!"

Smittionary
"Not your ordinary dictionary"
To get the best effect, say the italicized word(s) slowly

Word: marijuana

True definition: weed that is smoked

My definition: including your friend Mary

Sentence: "Hey, guys, wait! Let me see if *marijuana* go with you!"

Word: marinate

True definition: to soak or season meat before cooking

My definition: talking to your friend that is about to marry a guy named Nathaniel

Sentence: "Are you sure you want to *marinate*, or are you having second thoughts?"

Word: marmalade

True definition: jelly with fruit pieces inside

My definition: your mother taking a rest

Sentence: "I could tell she was tired 'cause *marmalade* down for three hours!"

Word: masseur

True definition: a man who practices massage therapy

My definition: a household utility

Sentence: "My water bill was high, but *masseur* bill was low this month!"

Smittionary
"Not your ordinary dictionary"
To get the best effect, say the italicized word(s) slowly

Word: mastectomy

True definition: removal of some or all of the breast

My definition: finding an error as in tax preparation

Sentence: "He hasn't made a mistake in years but missing a dependent sounds like a *mastectomy*!"

Word: mastery

True definition: a professional in a skill or competition

My definition: no deviation from your statement

Sentence: "I don't care if you believe me or not. That's *mastery*, and I'm sticking to it!"

Word: mastigophoran

True definition: any of a subphylum of proto-zoans comprising forms with flagella and including many often treated as algae

My definition: a famous golfer after he got caught cheating

Sentence: "When he got chased with a golf club, the *mastigophoran* to avoid getting hit!"

Smittionary
"Not your ordinary dictionary"
To get the best effect, say the italicized word(s) slowly

Word: matinees

True definition: performances or movies shown in the daytime or afternoon

My definition: bragging about your great grades in college

Sentence: "I'm not bragging, but *matinees* will get me on the dean's list!"

Word: matricide

True definition: one that murders his mother

My definition: a sleeping item

Sentence: "That mover was too strong because he ripped the handle right out of the *matricide*!"

Word: matriculate

True definition: to enroll as a member as a body as in college

My definition: a tardy prostitute

Sentence: "Julie, *matriculate* for your appointment, and I'm docking your pay!"

Word: matrix

True definition: something within which something else originates or develops

My definition: a female con named May

Smittionary
"Not your ordinary dictionary"
To get the best effect, say the italicized word(s) slowly

Sentence: "He got conned out of ten thousand dollars! Looks like *matrix* another man out of his money!"

Word: matter
True definition: subject at hand or a substance
My definition: has been introduced
Sentence: "He asked me if I have met his sister, and I said yes, I *matter* yesterday!"

Word: mattress
True definition: a fabric-covered sleeping apparatus
My definition: female bridal attire
Sentence: "I cannot wait to get married because *mattress* is simply beautiful!"

Word: mature
True definition: having completed natural growth and development
My definition: to fuss at
Sentence: "She knows she was wrong, so I *mature* out good when I see her again!"

Word: Maui
True definition: a Hawaiian island
My definition: a marriage proposal

Smittionary
"Not your ordinary dictionary"
To get the best effect, say the italicized word(s) slowly

Sentence: "I love her so much! I think I'll ask her to *Maui* me!"

Word: mayflower
True definition: any of various spring-blooming plants
My definition: a baking assistant
Sentence: "I will knead the dough, and Johnny, you *mayflower* the cake pan."

Word: mayhem
True definition: needless or willful damage or violence
My definition: a respectful greeting for an elder female
Sentence: "I told Mrs. Jenkens, 'Yes, *mayhem*. I will take out your garbage for you!'"

Word: mayonnaise
True definition: dressing made of egg yolks, vegetable oils, and vinegar
My definition: our family
Sentence: "We don't have much money, but *mayonnaise* kids of mine do the best we can!"

Smittionary
"Not your ordinary dictionary"
To get the best effect, say the italicized word(s) slowly

Word: mayor

True definition: an elected official to lead a
city or town

My definition: undecided

Sentence: "I don't know. I *mayor* may not go
to the dance tonight!"

Word: maypole

True definition: a tall flower-wreathed pole
forming a center for May Day sports and
dances

My definition: a type of tree or flavoring

Sentence: "I love *maypole* syrup on my pancakes!"

Word: McAdoo

True definition: someone's last name

My definition: praising Michael

Sentence: "Everyone has tried, but no one has
mastered the dance moves that *McAdoo*!"

Word: mealy-mouthed

True definition: not plain and straightforward

My definition: Mickey and Minnie's daughter

Sentence: "Hey, Goofy! Have you met our
daughter, *mealy-mouthed*?"

Smittionary
"Not your ordinary dictionary"
To get the best effect, say the italicized word(s) slowly

Word: meander

True definition: a winding path or course

My definition: me and someone

Sentence: "She's gonna be in more trouble by the time *meander* momma gets ahold of her!"

Word: measles

True definition: a viral infection

My definition: rockets for destruction

Sentence: "The building blew all to pieces when the *measles* hit it!"

Word: mecca

True definition: a place regarded as a center for a specified group, activity, or interest

My definition: to construct

Sentence: "I'm hungry. I think I'll *mecca* peanut butter sandwich!"

Word: medalist

True definition: a recipient of a medal or award

My definition: written-down wants

Sentence: "I can't wait to see Santa. I *medalist* of all the toys I want already!"

Smittionary
"Not your ordinary dictionary"
To get the best effect, say the italicized word(s) slowly

Word: media

True definition: a network that advertises or communicates

My definition: more meat

Sentence: "Those steaks we had last week were *media* than these skimpy ones!"

Word: meditate

True definition: to engage in reflection

My definition: a forced culinary sample

Sentence: "That dish she prepared was so bad the chef *meditate* it for herself!"

Word: Mejico

True definition: Mexico pronounced differently

My definition: asking permission

Sentence: "Mrs. Johnson, there's a dance tonight, and we want John to go. *Mejico* with us?"

Word: melanoma

True definition: a tumor containing dark pigment

My definition: explaining something to Mel

Sentence: "*Melanoma* work isn't the best sometimes, but I try to do a good job!"

Smittionary
"Not your ordinary dictionary"
To get the best effect, say the italicized word(s) slowly

Word: melee
True definition: a confused struggle
My definition: to sit something somewhere
Sentence: "That's the new rug. You *melee* it over in the next room."

Word: mellifluous
True definition: having a smooth rich flow
My definition: free airline tickets from Mellie
Sentence: "We had to go because *mellifluous* first class in her private jet!"

Word: menu
True definition: a list of restaurant dishes
My definition: guys
Sentence: "You've dated so much I bet you can't remember half the *menu* met!"

Word: menudo
True definition: a tripe stew seasoned with chili peppers
My definition: an apparatus with a doorknob
Sentence: "Hey, come and check out *menudo* I got from Lowes!"

Smittionary
"Not your ordinary dictionary"
To get the best effect, say the italicized word(s) slowly

Word: meringue

True definition: pie topping made with egg whites

My definition: jewelry worn on finger

Sentence: "My wife is gonna kill me. I think I lost *meringue*!"

Word: mermaid

True definition: a female with a fishlike lower body

My definition: biblical fragrance

Sentence: "I liked the frankincense, but that *mermaid* the room smell very good!"

Word: mesh

True definition: the fabric of a net

My definition: disarray

Sentence: "I dropped the flour on the floor and made a huge *mesh* of things!"

Word: metaphor

True definition: figurative language or a symbol of something similar

My definition: a date

Sentence: "She accepted my invitation, so I *metaphor* dinner and a movie!"

Smittionary
"Not your ordinary dictionary"
To get the best effect, say the italicized word(s) slowly

Word: meteor

True definition: an atmospheric phenomenon

My definition: not lacking in substance

Sentence: "Please check to see if that chicken is *meteor* not!"

Word: Michiganite

True definition: a resident of Michigan

My definition: a goodbye phrase

Sentence: "She didn't talk long because it was her bedtime, but she did tell me I *Michiganite*!"

Word: mignon

True definition: a tender cut of steak

My definition: bored guys

Sentence: "If they are bored, *mignon* ten times a day!"

Word: mildew

True definition: discoloration caused by fungi

My definition: good food

Sentence: "I may just be hungry, but this *mildew* hit the right spot!"

Word: mineral

True definition: an inorganic substance

Smittionary
"Not your ordinary dictionary"
To get the best effect, say the italicized word(s) slowly

My definition: the male species

Sentence: "All women think that *mineral* the same!"

Word: miniaturize

True definition: to design or construct in a small size

My definition: observance

Sentence: "I knew you liked me the *miniaturize* glanced into mine!"

Word: Minneapolis

True definition: a city in Minnesota

My definition: cops that monitor small iPhone apps

Sentence: "I tried to download that illegal small app and got caught by the *Minneapolis*!"

Word: minute

True definition: sixty seconds

My definition: crafts with yarn

Sentence: "I know for a fact that some *minute* and others like to crochet!"

Word: misconduct

True definition: mismanagement or intentional wrongdoing

Smittionary
"Not your ordinary dictionary"
To get the best effect, say the italicized word(s) slowly

My definition: a lucky female prisoner

Sentence: "The guard broke up the fight with rubber bullets, but *misconduct* and didn't get hit!"

Word: misdemeanor

True definition: a crime less serious than a felony

My definition: avoiding a bad person

Sentence: "I'm glad you were a little late. You just *misdemeanor* twin by ten minutes!"

Word: misery

True definition: a state of great unhappiness and emotional distress

My definition: a state

Sentence: "Next year, I'm planning a trip to St. Louis, *misery*!"

Word: misjudge

True definition: to wrongly estimate

My definition: a female justice of the peace

Sentence: "The defendant said…'Ummm… *misjudge*, can you reduce my sentence?'"

Word: Mississippi

True definition: a state

Smittionary
"Not your ordinary dictionary"
To get the best effect, say the italicized word(s) slowly

My definition: a spill-proof baby cup

Sentence: "I know my baby won't miss his bottle, but he will definitely *Mississippi* cup!"

Word: missus

True definition: another word for wife

My definition: a lack of being with someone

Sentence: "You're acting bad now, but you're gonna *missus* when we're gone!"

Word: mistake

True definition: to make a wrong judgement

My definition: something a regretful vegetarian might say

Sentence: "These vegetables are okay for my diet, but I sure do *mistake* and potatoes to eat!"

Word: mister

True definition: how you address a man who is a stranger

My definition: a no-show

Sentence: "They will not schedule her again. This is the third time she *mister* appointment!"

Smittionary
"Not your ordinary dictionary"
To get the best effect, say the italicized word(s) slowly

Word: mistletoe

True definition: a Christmas plant used to get a kiss from someone

My definition: weapon destruction

Sentence: "After it hit, that *mistletoe* up everything within a five-hundred-foot radius!"

Word: mitosis

True definition: a process that takes place in the nucleus of a dividing cell

My definition: blaming your female sibling

Sentence: "Make sure I'm out of your way the next time. You just ran over *mitosis*!"

Word: Moabites

True definition: members of an ancient Semitic people related to the Hebrews

My definition: eating action

Sentence: "It takes a small child *Moabites* to chew his food than it does adults!"

Word: mobbish

True definition: crowds who like disorder or defiance

My definition: a pimp's moneymaker

Sentence: "I don't care how long she stays out there. *Mobbish* better have my money!"

Smittionary
"Not your ordinary dictionary"
To get the best effect, say the italicized word(s) slowly

Word: mocking

True definition: to imitate for ridicule

My definition: card player move

Sentence: "I won! *Mocking* beat your queen and your jack!"

Word: mode

True definition: a form or manner of expression

My definition: cut grass

Sentence: "Since it rained, I *mode* my yard three times!"

Word: modem

True definition: a device used to pair a computer with a phone line

My definition: cut grass

Sentence: "Three people had overgrown lawns, so I *modem* all!"

Word: modern

True definition: the present or up to date

My definition: my darn

Sentence: "I got a DUI and lost *modern* license!"

Word: modernize

True definition: to adopt modern ways

My definition: bad vision

Smittionary
"Not your ordinary dictionary"
To get the best effect, say the italicized word(s) slowly

Sentence: "I used to see very well until *modernize* went bad!"

Word: molasses
True definition: a thick brown syrup
My definition: young women
Sentence: "The party wasn't that good because there were *molasses* than lads that showed up!"

Word: moment
True definition: a minute portion or point of time
My definition: flavoring
Sentence: "That chewing gum needed *moment* in it!"

Word: money
True definition: currency
My definition: a bendable leg part
Sentence: "I fell on the ice and skinned *money*!"

Word: morbid
True definition: gruesome or grisly
My definition: a higher offer
Sentence: "Charlie won the auction because he had *morbid* experience!"

Smittionary
"Not your ordinary dictionary"
To get the best effect, say the italicized word(s) slowly

Word: morbidness

True definition: having symptoms of gruesomeness or gloominess

My definition: better at conducting business

Sentence: "Let Paul deal with them because he has *morbidness* experience than we do!"

Word: Moroccan

True definition: a native of Morocco

My definition: a music genre

Sentence: "The teens of the fifties and sixties listened to *Moroccan* roll music than kids of today!"

Word: morphogen

True definition: a diffusible chemical that exerts control by forming a gradient concentration

My definition: a higher liquor price

Sentence: "One liquor store is charging *morphogen* than the other ones!"

Word: morphometry

True definition: measurement of external form

My definition: an arborist purchase

Sentence: "The scientist paid me *morphometry* than it was worth!"

Smittionary
"Not your ordinary dictionary"
To get the best effect, say the italicized word(s) slowly

Word: morrow

True definition: the time immediately after a specified event

My definition: a straight line

Sentence: "I think *morrow* of corn stalks is straighter than farmer Joe's row!"

Word: motel

True definition: an establishment for lodging and the rooms are usually close to parking

My definition: a larger rear end

Sentence: "She had plastic surgery because she came back with *motel* than she left with!"

Word: motif

True definition: a single or repeated design or color

My definition: molars

Sentence: "Grandaddy smiles a lot more since he got *motif* in his mouth!"

Word: motto

True definition: a short expression of a guiding principle

My definition: a part of my foot

Smittionary
"Not your ordinary dictionary"
To get the best effect, say the italicized word(s) slowly

Sentence: "I am limping because that car ran over *motto*!"

Word: mustache
True definition: shaped hair around the top of a man's lip
My definition: a hidden treasure
Sentence: "I'm glad those robbers didn't find *mustache* of money I hid!"

Word: mulatto
True definition: a person of mixed races, usually Black and White
My definition: gambling items
Sentence: "I am going to the store to buy *mulatto* tickets!"

Word: mullet
True definition: a hairstyle that is short on the sides and long in the back
My definition: to allow
Sentence: "Since the kids have been good, I *mullet* them go to the park today!"

Word: mystifier
True definition: someone who practices mysterious or obscure ways

Smittionary
"Not your ordinary dictionary"
To get the best effect, say the italicized word(s) slowly

My definition: a close call

Sentence: "I was very lucky because I *mystifier* truck by inches when I slammed on my brakes!"

Word: myth

True definition: an unfounded or false notion

My definition: a lady's title

Sentence: "It was really good to see my former teacher, *myth* Johnson!"

Smittionary
"Not your ordinary dictionary"
To get the best effect, say the italicized word(s) slowly

N

Word: nachos
True definition: tortilla chips
   with melted cheese
My definition: not belonging
   to you

Sentence: "Johnny, put those
   watches back because they are *nachos*!"

Word: naive
True definition: deficient in worldly wisdom
   or informed judgement
My definition: scolding the first lady of the
   earth
Sentence: "You had a conversation with a ser-
   pent? *Naïve*, you know better than that!"

Word: Nantucket
True definition: an island in Massachusetts
My definition: Nan, the kleptomaniac

Smittionary
"Not your ordinary dictionary"
To get the best effect, say the italicized word(s) slowly

Sentence: "There was twenty-five dollars sitting on my dresser, but I believe *Nantucket!*"

Word: napkin

True definition: folded cloth or paper used to wipe hands or mouth

My definition: benefits of sleep

Sentence: "I always say that a good *napkin* calm the rest of your day!"

Word: narrow

True definition: slender, thin, not wide

My definition: self-powering a boat

Sentence: "I refuse to be stuck in the middle of the lake. *Narrow* this boat so we can get ashore!"

Word: NASCAR

True definition: National Association for Stock Car Auto Racing

My definition: a compliment

Sentence: "Hey, George. That Porsche of yours sure is a *NASCAR!*"

Word: Nashville

True definition: a city in Tennessee

My definition: a good cut of meat

Smittionary
"Not your ordinary dictionary"
To get the best effect, say the italicized word(s) slowly

Sentence: "I want one of those *Nashville* steaks with a baked potato and a salad!"

Word: nausea
True definition: stomach distress with a distaste for food
My definition: family knowledge
Sentence: "George here says he *nausea* whole family!"

Word: nauseate
True definition: to become affected with stomach distress
My definition: a hungry female
Sentence: "Did she pick with her food, you ask? *Nauseate* everything on her plate!"

Word: nautical
True definition: related to or associated with seamen, navigation, or ships
My definition: absence of haulers
Sentence: "The mining operation was closed today because there was *nautical* truck in sight!"

Smittionary
"Not your ordinary dictionary"
To get the best effect, say the italicized word(s) slowly

Word: Navajo

True definition: a member of an American Indian people

My definition: gardening tips

Sentence: "And tip number four... *Navajo* your garden when the ground is hard!"

Word: navigator

True definition: one who navigates or guides

My definition: a letdown for a possible suitor

Sentence: "Give it up, Hank. You'll *navigator* to go out with you!"

Word: neon

True definition: a gas used in lighting

My definition: a leg part

Sentence: "I hit my *neon* the coffee table again!"

Word: neurosis

True definition: a mental and emotional disorder of a personality

My definition: flowers

Sentence: "She was mad at me, but I *neurosis* delivered to her would make things better!"

Smittionary
"Not your ordinary dictionary"
To get the best effect, say the italicized word(s) slowly

Word: newbie
True definition: a newcomer to cyberspace
My definition: an insect
Sentence: "The minute I killed the first bee, a
newbie tried to sting me!"

Word: New Hampshire
True definition: a US State
My definition: meat from a pig
Sentence: "The old ham didn't taste that
good, but the *New Hampshire* did have a
lot of flavor!"

Word: newlywed
True definition: a person recently married
My definition: knowledge of your friend Lee's
nuptials
Sentence: "I meant to tell you, but I *newlywed*
his high-school sweetheart last week!"

Word: Nicholas
True definition: a boy's name
My definition: demands
Sentence: "I want a twenty-five-cent raise,
and I will not take a *Nicholas*!"

Smittionary
"Not your ordinary dictionary"
To get the best effect, say the italicized word(s) slowly

Word: Nicolson
True definition: someone's last name
My definition: teaching your son about coins
Sentence: "That's not a quarter. That's just a
 Nicolson!"

Word: Nineveh
True definition: ancient city of Assyria
My definition: avoiding a question
Sentence: "I really think that information is
 Nineveh business!"

Word: nirvana
True definition: a place or state of oblivion to
 care, pain, or external reality
My definition: internal organs
Sentence: "I will not go to that dentist again!
 He cut a *nirvana* blood vessel at the same
 time!"

Word: Nissan
True definition: a car company
My definition: leg parts
Sentence: "Johnny fell and skinned his *Nissan*
 the sidewalk!"

Smittionary
"Not your ordinary dictionary"
To get the best effect, say the italicized word(s) slowly

Word: nitwit

True definition: a scatterbrained or stupid person

My definition: sweater-making tools

Sentence: "What kind of needles do you *nitwit*?"

Word: Noah

True definition: Biblical patriarch that built the ark

My definition: familiar with

Sentence: "Does anybody *Noah* good steak restaurant I can try?"

Word: Nobel

True definition: a prize for philanthropy

My definition: missing a sound object

Sentence: "We had to knock hard on the big door because there was *Nobel* to ring!"

Word: nobility

True definition: the quality or state of being noble in character, quality, or rank

My definition: unable to perform

Sentence: "He was useless around the house! He had *nobility* to do anything constructive!"

Smittionary
"Not your ordinary dictionary"
To get the best effect, say the italicized word(s) slowly

Word: nocturn

True definition: a principal division of the office of matins (prayers)

My definition: hitting on a door

Sentence: "She was surprised how that one *nocturn* into so many opportunities!"

Word: nodder

True definition: a person that makes a quick downward motion of their head

My definition: not her

Sentence: "We all know that dating is *nodder* strong suit!"

Word: node

True definition: a discrete mass of one kind of tissue enclosed in a different kind of tissue

My definition: familiar with

Sentence: "I put my hand up because I *node* what the answer was!"

Word: Noel

True definition: a Christmas carol

My definition: missing a letter of the alphabet

Sentence: "He's wrong! There's *Noel* in the word *crow*!"

Smittionary
"Not your ordinary dictionary"
To get the best effect, say the italicized word(s) slowly

Word: noggin

True definition: a small mug or cup or a person's head

My definition: hitting a door

Sentence: "We've been *noggin* on your door for ten minutes, and you finally answered!"

Word: noise

True definition: loud, confused, or senseless sound

My definition: a missing letter of the alphabet

Sentence: "I don't believe there are *noise* in the word *still*!"

Word: noisy

True definition: full of sound

My definition: difficult or hard

Sentence: "Sam. There is *noisy* way to tell you this, but you are not going with us!"

Word: nomad

True definition: an individual who roams about

My definition: getting an understanding

Sentence: "We have explained the conditions so there won't be *nomad* tourists!"

Smittionary
"Not your ordinary dictionary"
To get the best effect, say the italicized word(s) slowly

Word: nominee

True definition: a person proposed for a job or task

My definition: part of the leg

Sentence: "I sat on that ground for three hours, and *nominee* is stiff!"

Word: no-par

True definition: having no nominal value

My definition: no electricity

Sentence: "All the lights went out in the house today. Looks like we will have *no-par* for a while!"

Word: normalizer

True definition: one that makes things normal

My definition: a habitual fib teller

Sentence: "I know she's your friend, but *normalizer* butt off about everything!"

Word: Norwalk

rue definition: a city in Connecticut

My definition: balance difficulties

Sentence: "You cannot run *Norwalk* on solid ice!"

Smittionary
"Not your ordinary dictionary"
To get the best effect, say the italicized word(s) slowly

Word: nosy

True definition: meddlesome

My definition: a missing letter of the alphabet

Sentence: "Even though it sounds like it, there is *nosy* in the word *xylophone*!"

Word: nosing

True definition: the rounded edge of a stair tread

My definition: lack of excitement

Sentence: "There is just *nosing* in their relationship!"

Word: notarize

True definition: acknowledge or attest as a notary public

My definition: patriotic

Sentence: "Everyone should *notarize* for the singing of the national anthem!"

Word: notate

True definition: to mark down with characters, words, or signs

My definition: food comparison

Sentence: "This cake is okay, but it *notate* like my granny's cakes!"

Smittionary
"Not your ordinary dictionary"
To get the best effect, say the italicized word(s) slowly

Word: nourish

True definition: to promote the growth of

My definition: a hope or want

Sentence: "I am your personal genie. *Nourish* is too hard for me to fulfill!"

Word: nowhere

True definition: to no place

My definition: hardly any use

Sentence: "Johnny is growing so fast he really didn't get *nowhere* from his clothes!"

Word: nuance

True definition: a subtle quality

My definition: new kinfolk

Sentence: "I met many *nuance* and uncles at the family reunion."

Word: nuclear

True definition: of or relating to the atomic nucleus

My definition: understandable

Sentence: "I now have a *nuclear* vision on the company's direction."

Word: nugget

True definition: a solid lump

Smittionary
"Not your ordinary dictionary"
To get the best effect, say the italicized word(s) slowly

My definition: a direct order

Sentence: "I am not going to argue with you! *Nugget* in the car so we can go!"

Word: nuisance

True definition: one that is annoying, unpleasant, or obnoxious

My definition: not feasible

Sentence: "He bought a boat and can't pay his rent? That makes *nuisance* to me!"

Word: numerators

True definition: the top number of a fraction

My definition: NFL team disappointment

Sentence: "For some reason, I *numerators* wouldn't make the playoffs!"

Word: numerical

True definition: relating to numbers

My definition: a divine event

Sentence: "I am always waiting and hoping for a *numerical* to happen!"

Word: nutmeg

True definition: a spice

My definition: a crazy friend named Megan

Smittionary
"Not your ordinary dictionary"
To get the best effect, say the italicized word(s) slowly

Sentence: "I went to the party, and that *nut-meg* drank a whole bottle of whiskey by herself!"

Word: nutter
True definition: another word for nut
My definition: additional
Sentence: "They told me that your sister is about to have a *nutter* baby!"

Smittionary
"Not your ordinary dictionary"
To get the best effect, say the italicized word(s) slowly

O

Word: oasis

True definition: a fertile or green area in a desert

My definition: greeting your female sibling

Sentence: "*Oasis*. I didn't see you standing there!"

Word: obedience

True definition: an act or instance of obeying

My definition: slow to understand

Sentence: "I said to him, '*obedience* if you want to, but you are smarter than that!'"

Word: obey

True definition: to conform to or comply with

My definition: pleading with your girlfriend

Sentence: "Then Frank said, '*Obey*, you know I need you!'"

Smittionary
"Not your ordinary dictionary"
To get the best effect, say the italicized word(s) slowly

Word: occasion

True definition: an occurrence or condition that brings something about

My definition: spicy, seasoned cooked food

Sentence: "He had to be from Louisiana because he prepared *occasion* meal for us!"

Word: occlude

True definition: to close up or block off

My definition: to inform

Sentence: "He didn't know what was happening, so *occlude* him in on the process!"

Word: occult

True definition: to shut off from view or exposure

My definition: past tense of catch

Sentence: "We went fishing and *occult* five bass and three blue gill!"

Word: occur

True definition: to come into existence

My definition: to feel interest or concern

Sentence: "I wanted to show her how much *occur* about her!"

Smittionary
"Not your ordinary dictionary"
To get the best effect, say the italicized word(s) slowly

Word: oddity

True definition: the quality or state of being odd

My definition: a drink made by filtering water through bags

Sentence: "How was our drinks? *Oddity* was very good even without sugar and lemon!"

Word: Odessa

True definition: a city in Texas

My definition: a description

Sentence: "The red thing there? *Odessa* bell that's been painted!"

Word: odeum

True definition: a theatre or concert hall

My definition: indebted

Sentence: "I need to go to the bank because I *odeum* twenty dollars!"

Word: odor

True definition: a scent or smell

My definition: indebted to a female

Sentence: "Mary stopped speaking to me because I *odor* some money!"

Smittionary
"Not your ordinary dictionary"
To get the best effect, say the italicized word(s) slowly

Word: odorant
True definition: a scented or smelly substance
My definition: monthly house-payment due
Sentence: "My landlord is patient because he never mentioned that we *odorant* for last month!"

Word: odorize
True definition: to produce a scent
My definition: seasoned sight
Sentence: "John didn't see the small sign because he has much *odorize* than we do!"

Word: odorous
True definition: fragrant
My definition: to lead without permission
Sentence: "We won't play with him anymore because he always tries to *odorous* around!"

Word: odyssey
True definition: a long wandering or voyage
My definition: suggested viewing
Sentence: "Hey, Mike. You really *odyssey* that new crime movie!"

Smittionary
"Not your ordinary dictionary"
To get the best effect, say the italicized word(s) slowly

Word: offense

True definition: the state of being insulted or
    morally outraged

My definition: a yard separator

Sentence: "That dog keeps getting in my yard,
    so I am going to get *offense* tomorrow!"

Word: offender

True definition: a violator of a law or rule

My definition: a car part

Sentence: "I will go to the junkyard to find
    offender for my car."

Word: offering

True definition: a contribution as to a church

My definition: a sign that a relationship is over

Sentence: "As soon as he said it was over, she
    took *offering* and threw it at him!"

Word: officiate

True definition: to perform a ceremony

My definition: sick from seafood

Sentence: "She threw up three times probably
    from *officiate* earlier!"

Word: off-kilter

True definition: not in perfect balance

Smittionary
"Not your ordinary dictionary"
To get the best effect, say the italicized word(s) slowly

My definition: a product that works

Sentence: "She was happy that *off-kilter* mosquitoes like it advertised!"

Word: oink

True definition: a noise a pig makes

My definition: blink of one eye for attention

Sentence: "He told me that all it takes is *oink* of an eye, and I'm his!"

Word: olive

True definition: a fruit that can be eaten and produces oil for cooking

My definition: where I dwell

Sentence: "I was going to join the gym, but *olive* too far away!"

Word: Olympiad

True definition: one of the four-year intervals between Olympic games celebration

My definition: a lame unsteady walk

Sentence: "My uncle Bert was known best for *Olympiad* when he was younger."

Word: ombudsperson

True definition: one that investigates reported complaints for settlement

Smittionary
"Not your ordinary dictionary"
To get the best effect, say the italicized word(s) slowly

My definition: Bud's contact

Sentence: "If he needs things done, *ombudsperson* he calls!"

Word: omelet

True definition: eggs made with ham, onions, peppers folded in half

My definition: allowance

Sentence: "Since you have been good this week, *omelet* you go skating tonight!"

Word: omen

True definition: occurrence believed to indicate a future event

My definition: senior males

Sentence: "That club is just a bunch of *omen* sitting around, telling tales!"

Word: onomatology

True definition: the science or study of the origin and forms of proper names

My definition: giving an award to someone other than a short gangster

Sentence: "My friend is seven foot one, so let's not forget to *onomatology* with an award too!"

Smittionary
"Not your ordinary dictionary"
To get the best effect, say the italicized word(s) slowly

Word: Ophelia

True definition: a female name

My definition: suggestion for liquid consumption

Sentence: "So you drank all your Moscato, and you're mad? *Ophelia* glass back up and be quiet!"

Word: opiate

True definition: a drug containing opium to induce sleep

My definition: Andy's son's appetite

Sentence: "He was hungry because *opiate* three helpings of dumplings!"

Word: opossum

True definition: an animal that has a pointed snout that can play dead for protection

My definition: speeding around another driver

Sentence: "Should you go around that slow driver, you ask? *Opossum* up already!"

Word: Oppenheimer

True definition: a physicist

My definition: a small nailing tool

Sentence: "You don't need a big hammer for the little nail. *Oppenheimer* will work!"

Smittionary
"Not your ordinary dictionary"
To get the best effect, say the italicized word(s) slowly

Word: opponent

True definition: one who takes an opposite position

My definition: in the know

Sentence: "If there is anything interesting going on, George is *opponent* quickly!"

Word: opposed

True definition: resisted or counterbalanced

My definition: expected to

Sentence: "As soon as the guests arrive, *opposed* to show them their rooms!"

Word: optimize

True definition: to make as perfect, effective, or functional as possible

My definition: a full workload

Sentence: "I can't handle another task. I'm already *optimize* in paperwork from last week!"

Word: optimum

True definition: the greatest degree attained under specific conditions

My definition: leaving a decision to your mom

Sentence: "Well, it's really *optimum* where she wants to eat tomorrow!"

Smittionary
"Not your ordinary dictionary"
To get the best effect, say the italicized word(s) slowly

Word: oregano

True definition: a spice for cooking

My definition: a former president's knowledge

Sentence: "The address to the White House?
  Oregano how to get there!"

Word: Orient

True definition: the East or anything belonging to the Eastern world

My definition: to pay to stay in a house or
  apartment

Sentence: "Does anyone know of a good place
  to buy *Orient*?"

Word: Oriental

True definition: one who is a native of east Asia

My definition: an item or service that is leased
  for money

Sentence: "No, that's not my new car! It's just
  Oriental car!"

Word: orifice

True definition: an opening as a vent, mouth,
  or hole

My definition: unsure

Sentence: "Question number 4. I'm not sure
  if it's false *orifice* true!"

Smittionary
"Not your ordinary dictionary"
To get the best effect, say the italicized word(s) slowly

Word: origin

True definition: the point at which something begins or is started

My definition: an alcoholic drink

Sentence: "Are you going to order a Bloody Mary *origin* and tonic?"

Word: oriole

True definition: a type of bird

My definition: not fake

Sentence: "This time, she went on *oriole* date with a nice guy!"

Word: orismological

True definition: a defined technical term

My definition: comparing wits

Sentence: "Are you going to accept his bad choice, *orismological* answer better?"

Word: orthodontics

True definition: dentistry dealing with irregular teeth

My definition: blood-sucking bugs

Sentence: "Keep some bug spray handy, *orthodontics* will bite you!"

Smittionary
"Not your ordinary dictionary"
To get the best effect, say the italicized word(s) slowly

Word: orthodox

True definition: conforming to established doctrine

My definition: loading areas beside an ocean or river

Sentence: "Keep the large ships away, *orthodox* will be congested quickly!"

Word: Osborn

True definition: a famous paleontologist or someone's last name

My definition: your birthplace

Sentence: "I live in Texas but *Osborn* in Mississippi!"

Word: Oscar

True definition: a golden statue for movie achievement

My definition: to make a request

Sentence: "I don't know if she wants to go, but I'll *Oscar.*"

Word: oscillate

True definition: to move back and forth between two points

My definition: tardy

Smittionary
"Not your ordinary dictionary"
To get the best effect, say the italicized word(s) slowly

Sentence: "*Oscillate* for the party I might as well stay home!"

Word: oscillogram
True definition: a record made by an oscillo-graph (waveform recording instrument)
My definition: drug-trafficking pride
Sentence: "You are such an amateur. *Oscillogram* of coke every hour!"

Word: Oshawa
true definition: Canadian city
My definition: something to prove
Sentence: "Mary thinks she can tell me what to do, but *Oshawa* who's boss!"

Word: Oslo
True definition: capital of Norway
My definition: insufficient amount
Sentence: "I'm glad I checked out my car because *Oslo* on oil!"

Smittionary
"Not your ordinary dictionary"
To get the best effect, say the italicized word(s) slowly

P

Word: pack rat
True definition: a hoarder
My definition: a proper way to place items
Sentence: "I told her to learn to *pack rat* or use a bigger suitcase!"

Word: paddy wagon
True definition: an enclosed vehicle for transporting prisoners
My definition: a happy dog
Sentence: "When his owners come home, they always see *paddy wagon* her tail!"

Word: painful
True definition: an annoying hurt
My definition: no credit-card balance
Sentence: "I always use my credit card and *painful* at the end of every month!"

Smittionary
"Not your ordinary dictionary"
To get the best effect, say the italicized word(s) slowly

Word: palace

True definition: official residence of a king or queen

My definition: stacking

Sentence: "Do you still want to *palace* wood in the barn?"

Word: palatable

True definition: agreeable or acceptable to the mind

My definition: setting a table for dinner

Sentence: "Along with a plate and fork, *palatable* and spoon for soup also!"

Word: paleoanthropology

True definition: branch of anthropology dealing with fossils

My definition: correcting a wrong with money owed to Leo

Sentence: "Since you miscalculated, I want you to *paleoanthropology* his way for being wrong!"

Word: paleoecology

True definition: study of characteristics of ancient environments

My definitions: fair treatment for Leo at bingo

Smittionary
"Not your ordinary dictionary"
To get the best effect, say the italicized word(s) slowly

Sentence: "After confirming, they will *paleo-ecology* 45 on the last game to win!"

Word: palimony
True definition: court-ordered payment to one member of a unmarried couple
My definition: wad of cash
Sentence: "He is loaded because he always brings a *palimony* to the racetrack!"

Word: palladium
True definition: an element that is used in electrical contacts
My definition: to trick or con someone
Sentence: "That con artist *palladium* like a fool on that business deal!"

Word: pallbearer
True definition: a person who helps carry a coffin
My definition: a daddy grizzly
Sentence: "I went hiking and saw a *pallbearer*, maw bear, and a baby bear!"

Word: Panama
True definition: a country
My definition: culinary skills

Smittionary
"Not your ordinary dictionary"
To get the best effect, say the italicized word(s) slowly

Sentence: "You haven't had anything until you've had a *Panama* soup beans!"

Word: pandemonium
True definition: a wild uproar
My definition: making a bear attack
Sentence: "They haven't been back to the zoo since that worker sicced the *pandemonium*!"

Word: papa
True definition: another word for father
My definition: to bust something
Sentence: "He actually asked me to *papa* zit for him!"

Word: paparazzo
True definition: photographer who pursues celebrities for money
My definition: your deceased father decaying
Sentence: "The undertaker said that *paparazzo* fast they couldn't preserve him!"

Word: paperboy
True definition: a boy who delivers newspapers
My definition: equal distributions of funds
Sentence: "No one makes more than the other. I believe in equal *paperboy*."

Smittionary
"Not your ordinary dictionary"
To get the best effect, say the italicized word(s) slowly

Word: parade

True definition: floats, bands, and attractions that stroll down the street for crowds

My definition: a SWAT person's pay

Sentence: "I heard that SWAT members get 1,000 dollars *parade* on drug houses!"

Word: paradigms

True definition: examples or patterns

My definition: two ten-cent pieces

Sentence: "He's so dumb he mistook a pair of quarters for a *paradigms.*"

Word: paradise

True definition: a place or state of bliss

My definition: two square objects with dots used in gambling

Sentence: "When the officers raided the crap game, all they found was a *paradise.*"

Word: paralyze

True definition: to stun or to make powerless or ineffective

My definition: two fibs

Sentence: "Those two don't know what really happened! They just told you a *paralyze!*"

Smittionary
"Not your ordinary dictionary"
To get the best effect, say the italicized word(s) slowly

Word: paranoia

True definition: psychosis characterized by systemized delusions

My definition: recognition

Sentence: "Just keep talking to them, and that *paranoia* by your voice!"

Word: paraphrase

True definition: a restatement of a text

My definition: two tears or rips

Sentence: "This could have started a fire because you have a *paraphrase* in your electrical wire!"

Word: parasite

True definition: an organism living in, with, or on another organism

My definition: disgust with a couple

Sentence: "They are both married to other people. That *parasite* to be seen!"

Word: parasol

True definition: lightweight umbrella used for shade

My definition: a couple

Sentence: "That looks like the same *parasol* the other day!"

Smittionary
"Not your ordinary dictionary"
To get the best effect, say the italicized word(s) slowly

Word: parch

True definition: to toast under dry heat

My definition: an extension to a house where people can sit

Sentence: "Momma said we can't get off the front *parch*."

Word: parent

True definition: a mom or dad

My definition: monthly installment for a house or apartment

Sentence: "I would move out, but I don't want to *parent* just yet!"

Word: parodies

True definition: a feeble or ridiculous imitation

My definition: two of something

Sentence: "I think I am going to buy a *parodies* shoes!"

Word: parole

True definition: a conditional release of a prisoner

My definition: a quantity

Sentence: "This toilet paper is only fifty cents *parole*!"

Smittionary
"Not your ordinary dictionary"
To get the best effect, say the italicized word(s) slowly

Word: parrot

True definition: a tropical bird that can talk

My definition: to put one thing with another thing

Sentence: "To make it plural, just *parrot* with another!"

Word: pasteurize

True definition: to sterilize as in milk

My definition: not seen

Sentence: "That bird flew *pasteurize* so fast I got scared!"

Word: pastoring

True definition: serving as a spiritual advisor

My definition: handing jewelry to someone

Sentence: "When the preacher asked for it, the best man *pastoring* to him in the wedding!"

Word: pauperize

True definition: to reduce to poverty

My definition: bulging pupils

Sentence: "Sally is weird. One day, I saw her *pauperize* out then pop them back in!"

Smittionary
"Not your ordinary dictionary"
To get the best effect, say the italicized word(s) slowly

Word: Pawtucket

True definition: a city in Rhode Island

My definition: blaming your father

Sentence: "If you are looking for the last Pop-Tart, I think *Pawtucket*!"

Word: pediatric

True definition: medical care relating to the care of children

My definition: letting Pete know he's outdated

Sentence: "Pick a card? Really? *Pediatric* is so old and predictable!"

Word: pedicure

True definition: care of the feet, toes, and toenails

My definition: therapeutic animal

Sentence: "A nice little *pedicure* loneliness especially with older people."

Word: peeper

True definition: one who watches someone

My definition: urine amount

Sentence: "The nurse was only requiring two ounces of *peeper* patient."

Smittionary
"Not your ordinary dictionary"
To get the best effect, say the italicized word(s) slowly

Word: Pekinese

True definition: Chinese dialect of Beijing

My definition: looking at food with hunger

Sentence: "I'm ready for a snack. I've been *Pekinese* blackberries all morning!"

Word: pentagram

True definition: a five-pointed star used as a magic or occult symbol

My definition: drug crime charge

Sentence: "After he talked to the cops, they *pentagram* of coke charge on him!"

Word: Pentecost

True definition: Christian feast on the seventh Sunday after Easter

My definition: left with the bill

Sentence: "The IRS always tries to *Pentecost* of higher taxes on the consumer!"

Word: peon

True definition: a person usually walked on or overlooked

My definition: bad aim

Sentence: "Every time he uses my bathroom, there's always *peon* the floor!"

Smittionary
"Not your ordinary dictionary"
To get the best effect, say the italicized word(s) slowly

Word: percent

True definition: a portion based on one hundred

My definition: fragrance sales

Sentence: "The incense salesman was asking three dollars *percent* except for lilac!"

Word: per diem

True definition: based on use or service by the day

My definition: referring to

Sentence: "The river flows east to west *per diem* that know for sure!"

Word: perfectos

True definition: cigars that are thick in the middle and tapers at each end

My definition: feet joy

Sentence: "I was very happy that my baby had ten *perfectos*!"

Word: perky

True definition: briskly self-assured

My definition: buying a car accessory

Sentence: "Those foreign cars are expensive! They charge seventy-five dollars *perky* replacement!"

Smittionary
"Not your ordinary dictionary"
To get the best effect, say the italicized word(s) slowly

Word: permit
True definition: to make possible
My definition: softball glove cost
Sentence: "The sporting goods stores are charging fifty dollars *permit*!"

Word: perpetuate
True definition: to cause to last indefinitely
My definition: cannibal restaurant tally
Sentence: "One cannibal told his friend, 'You know, you are getting charged *perpetuate*!'"

Word: persecute
True definition: to harass or punish to cause suffering
My definition: admiring a woman's accessory
Sentence: "That *persecute*, I cannot put it down!"

Word: perspire
True definition: to sweat through the skin
My definition: voyeurism crime punishment
Sentence: "The judge gave ten years prison time *perspire* for illegal peeping!"

Word: peso
True definition: Spanish coin
My definition: terrible salary

Smittionary
"Not your ordinary dictionary"
To get the best effect, say the italicized word(s) slowly

Sentence: "I had to quit that job because they *peso* little!"

Word: pesticide
True definition: chemical used to destroy bugs
My definition: left- or right-hand area
Sentence: "The ball landed in the tall grass just *pesticide* of the house."

Word: pharaoh
True definition: ruler of ancient Egypt
My definition: a female boater
Sentence: "I saw *pharaoh* that little boat so fast she made waves!"

Word: pharmacist
True definition: a person that professionally dispenses drugs
My definition: money allotted for farmers
Sentence: "Mr. Brown qualified for the *pharmacist* grant after the flood."

Word: pharmacy
True definition: a place that dispenses medical drugs
My definition: a grade lower than a B

Smittionary
"Not your ordinary dictionary"
To get the best effect, say the italicized word(s) slowly

Sentence: "That test was hard, but I really worked *pharmacy* in that class!"

Word: Philadelphia
True definition: a city in Pennsylvania
My definition: empathizing with someone's phobia
Sentence: "I was scared, too, so it was easy to *Philadelphia* about haunted houses!"

Word: philandering
True definition: having relations with one or more women
My definition: Phil getting caught
Sentence: "She caught Phil red-handed, so she threw *philandering* he bought her out the door!"

Word: phobias
True definition: fears of particular objects or situations
My definition: alcoholic drinks
Sentence: "The bartender sent me and my three friends *phobias* on the house!"

Word: Phoebe
True definition: a female's name

Smittionary
"Not your ordinary dictionary"
To get the best effect, say the italicized word(s) slowly

My definition: a fixed charge complaint

Sentence: "I was going to hire the one lawyer, but his *Phoebe* too high!"

Word: phonogram

True definition: a character or symbol used to represent a word

My definition: quantity of drugs

Sentence: "They will never arrest me *phonogram* of cocaine!"

Word: photos

True definition: pictures taken with a camera

My definition: feet extensions

Sentence: "His foot got caught, and he lost *photos* in the machine!"

Word: physician

True definition: a person skilled in the art of healing

My definition: a slang way of speaking for casting a rod and reel or cane pole

Sentence: "Mizee and my fizather went *physician*, and I didn't even get a bizite!"

Smittionary
"Not your ordinary dictionary"
To get the best effect, say the italicized word(s) slowly

Word: piano

True definition: a musical instrument with eighty-eight keys

My definition: having to use the bathroom

Sentence: "You really have to *piano*, so go to the bathroom now!"

Word: piccolo

True definition: a small flute

My definition: a small number or quantity

Sentence: "Since you have the first choice, always *piccolo* number for starters!"

Word: picnic

True definition: an outing with food, usually outdoors

My definition: choosing a good teammate

Sentence: "John always has to *picnic* to be on his team because he is so good!"

Word: pictorial

True definition: relating to or consisting of pictures

My definition: a sensible choice

Sentence: "I am so glad he *pictorial* career this time!"

Smittionary
"Not your ordinary dictionary"
To get the best effect, say the italicized word(s) slowly

Word: picture

True definition: something painted, drawn, or photographed

My definition: chosen

Sentence: "Don't worry because we have already *picture* roommate for college!"

Word: pig latin

True definition: language derived from altered English

My definition: swine manners

Sentence: "That's cute how the large *pig latin* the babies eat first!"

Word: pilfer

True definition: to steal in small quantities

My definition: medication question

Sentence: "I forgot, Doc. Now what's this blue *pilfer* again?"

Word: pioneer

True definition: one of the first to settle into a territory

My definition: baked-goods location

Sentence: "Mrs. Baker always puts her baked *pioneer* the window so we can smell it!"

Smittionary
"Not your ordinary dictionary"
To get the best effect, say the italicized word(s) slowly

Word: piper

True definition: one that plays a musical pipe

My definition: distribution of baked goods

Sentence: "This Thanksgiving, they are only giving away one *piper* customer."

Word: pitcher

True definition: a container for holding liquids or a baseball player

My definition: to place somewhere

Sentence: "This is the last time I will tell you to *pitcher* toys away!"

Word: pituitaries

True definition: organs/glands connected to the brain

My definition: placement of Terry's items

Sentence: "For this art show, we will *pituitaries* paintings on display."

Word: pizza

True definition: dish made with dough, tomato sauce, cheese vegetables, and meat

My definition: a part or portion of

Sentence: "Momma always lets Daddy have the big *pizza* chicken!"

Smittionary
"Not your ordinary dictionary"
To get the best effect, say the italicized word(s) slowly

Word: plagiarize

True definition: to steal and pass off ideas or words of another as your own

My definition: to trick or fool

Sentence: "The magician *plagiarize* for a trick with those cards!"

Word: planet

True definition: any of the celestial bodies that revolve around the sun

My definition: preparation

Sentence: "To have a successful event, you have to *planet* in advance!"

Word: Plano

True definition: city in Texas

My definition: ordinary

Sentence: "All she wanted was a *Plano* cheeseburger, and they put everything on it!"

Word: plasma

True definition: the fluid part of blood

My definition: to put on something

Sentence: "I like this DJ. He always *plasma* favorite songs!"

Smittionary
"Not your ordinary dictionary"
To get the best effect, say the italicized word(s) slowly

Word: platinum

True definition: metal alloy that can be used in jewelry

My definition: to braid

Sentence: "The best way to style your wigs is to start *platinum* cornrow style!"

Word: Plato

True definition: a Greek philosopher

My definition: not a real toe

Sentence: "I moved my foot because he almost stepped on my *Plato*."

Word: plutonium

True definition: radioactive metallic element

My definition: famous theme-park dog and his crew

Sentence: "My kids weren't going to be happy until they saw *plutonium* at Disney World!"

Word: pneumonitis

True definition: inflammation of the lungs

My definition: a bad evening rescue

Sentence: "My friends made me laugh even though they *pneumonitis* ruined!"

Smittionary
"Not your ordinary dictionary"
To get the best effect, say the italicized word(s) slowly

Word: poach

True definition: to cook in simmering liquid

My definition: front or back area of a house you sit on

Sentence: "I told the kids not to leave the front *poach*."

Word: Poconos

True definition: mountains in Pennsylvania

My definition: meddlesome

Sentence: "Leave it to Sally to *Poconos* in everybody's business!"

Word: podium

True definition: a small platform used for speeches or public speaking

My definition: to dispense

Sentence: "Since they were drunk, the bartender refused to *podium* any more drinks!"

Word: poet

True definition: one who writes and narrates poetry

My definition: to dispense

Sentence: "I had a bug in my drink, so I made the waiter *poet* out and fix me another one!"

Smittionary
"Not your ordinary dictionary"
To get the best effect, say the italicized word(s) slowly

Word: poetry

True definition: the writings and verbal presentation of a poet

My definition: feeling sorry for a large plant with branches and leaves

Sentence: "After the 120-mph winds, that *poetry* didn't have a chance!"

Word: politics

True definition: the art or science of government

My definition: your friend Paula being nerve-wracking

Sentence: "I won't take her with me again because *politics* people off too much!"

Word: pomegranate

True definition: a red fruit or berry with a tart taste

My definition: telling your father about your countertops

Sentence: "Hey, *pomegranate* countertops came in today!"

Word: pompano

True definition: a small bluish or greenish fish

My definition: to put gas in

Smittionary
"Not your ordinary dictionary"
To get the best effect, say the italicized word(s) slowly

Sentence: "A woman shouldn't be *pompano* gas when a man is with her!"

Word: poncho
True definition: a waterproof garment with a hood
My definition: to hit
Sentence: "Never mess with a boxer. He can *poncho* lights out at any time!"

Word: ponder
True definition: to think and consider quietly and deeply
My definition: to hock
Sentence: "As soon as the engagement was called off, he *ponder* ring for two hundred dollars!"

Word: ponies
True definition: small horses
My definition: bendable leg parts
Sentence: "I can't walk very far because my *ponies* will start hurting!"

Word: populate
True definition: to occupy or inhabit
My definition: your tardy father

Smittionary
"Not your ordinary dictionary"
To get the best effect, say the italicized word(s) slowly

Sentence: "I said to pick me up at ten, not ten thirty. So *populate* again!"

Word: possum
True definition: a pointed-snout wild animal
My definition: buying for your father
Sentence: "We went to the mall and bought *possum* new shoes!"

Word: postmodern
True definition: of, relating to, or being an era after a modern one
My definition: displaying of something personal
Sentence: "That teacher didn't have to *postmodern* bad test score on the board!"

Word: potentiated
True definition: something that's made more effective or more active
My definition: faking food consumption
Sentence: "She threw that food away then tried to *potentiated* all up!"

Word: pressurize
True definition: to apply pressure to

Smittionary
"Not your ordinary dictionary"
To get the best effect, say the italicized word(s) slowly

My definition: placement of your vision instruments

Sentence: "The ophthalmologist said to *pressurize* against the vision machine."

Word: preventable

True definition: keeping something from happening

My definition: animal control

Sentence: "When in Spain, don't wear red if you want to *preventable* from charging!"

Word: primary

True definition: first in order of time or development

My definition: to pull someone away

Sentence: "That movie was so good no one could *primary* from the TV!"

Word: prior

True definition: earlier in time or order

My definition: release someone from a grip

Sentence: "The accident scared her so bad we couldn't *prior* fingers from the steering wheel!"

Smittionary
"Not your ordinary dictionary"
To get the best effect, say the italicized word(s) slowly

Word: probate

True definition: the judicial determination of the validity of a will

My definition: the best fishing lures

Sentence: "He's caught twenty-seven fish so far. He must be using *probate* on his line!"

Word: procedure

True definition: a particular way of accomplishing something or of acting

My definition: sowing grass

Sentence: "Always let a *procedure* lawn for the best results!"

Word: promise

True definition: a pledge to do something

My definition: a school dance

Sentence: "We're leaving because the senior *promise* boring this year!"

Word: propagator

True definition: someone who passes along something to their offspring

My definition: a brave animal-tamer move

Sentence: "That animal catcher is so brave. I saw him *propagator* on his back and wrestle it!"

Smittionary
"Not your ordinary dictionary"
To get the best effect, say the italicized word(s) slowly

Word: proper
True definition: decent or noble
My definition: lift or raise
Sentence: "She said when she gets home, she's
gonna *proper* feet up and relax!"

Word: psycho
True definition: a deranged person
My definition: a motorized vehicle
Sentence: "He just bought a new motor *psy-cho* and a helmet today!"

Word: puberty
True definition: preteen coming of age or first
stage of maturity
My definition: your friend Berty passing gas
Sentence: "*Puberty*! You stink!"

Word: pudding
True definition: a creamy soft dessert
My definition: installing or applying something
Sentence: "Are you *pudding* in your job appli-cation today?"

Word: pygmy
True definition: a dwarf
My definition: store request

Smittionary
"Not your ordinary dictionary"
To get the best effect, say the italicized word(s) slowly

Sentence: "When you go to the store, can you *pygmy* up some milk and butter, please?"

Word: pyromaniac
True definition: a person who has an obsession with fire
My definition: baked-goods fanatic
Sentence: "Does his love of bakeries make him a *pyromaniac*?"

Smittionary
"Not your ordinary dictionary"
To get the best effect, say the italicized word(s) slowly

Q

Word: quack

True definition: the sound that a duck makes

My definition: to break or split

Sentence: "Before you make breakfast, be sure to *quack* the eggs first!"

Word: quarterback

True definition: offensive leader of a football team

My definition: lost money

Sentence: "Who do I talk to to get my *quarterback* from this broken machine?"

Smittionary
"Not your ordinary dictionary"
To get the best effect, say the italicized word(s) slowly

R

Word: radar

True definition: a device that detects radio waves

My definition: eating up someone's food

Sentence: "Your friends cannot come over and *radar* refrigerator anymore!"

Word: raffle

True definition: a contest where a name is drawn for prizes

My definition: a long gun

Sentence: "Hey, paw. Git yer *raffle* 'cause thar's a bear in the yard!"

Word: radish

True definition: a round vegetable

My definition: to mount and travel in or on something

Smittionary
"Not your ordinary dictionary"
To get the best effect, say the italicized word(s) slowly

Sentence: "Today, I'm gonna *radish* horse, and I hope I don't get thrown off!"

Word: radon
True definition: a deadly odorless gas
My definition: repeat offender
Sentence: "I just got a call that *radon* got himself arrested again!"

Word: raisin
True definition: a small fruit from the prune family
My definition: incarcerated
Sentence: "Well, it's confirmed that *raisin* jail again!"

Word: ramus
True definition: a branch of the nerve
My definition: Lucky Ray
Sentence: "*Ramus* know the system really well because he's back out of jail already!"

Word: Randolph
True definition: a man's name
My definition: to expire or leave swiftly
Sentence: "He almost won a car, but time *Randolph* the clock!"

Smittionary
"Not your ordinary dictionary"
To get the best effect, say the italicized word(s) slowly

Word: random

True definition: something that happens without plan or purpose

My definition: completion

Sentence: "She entered five marathons and *random* all in record time!"

Word: Randy

True definition: a man's name

My definition: trot or sprint

Sentence: "She also *Randy* five marathons barefooted!"

Word: ransom

True definition: money paid to a kidnapper

My definition: to trot

Sentence: "I *ransom* and walked some, but I did complete the marathon!"

Word: raptor

True definition: a small dinosaur

My definition: covering a present

Sentence: "She was mad because he *raptor* gift in newspaper!"

Smittionary
"Not your ordinary dictionary"
To get the best effect, say the italicized word(s) slowly

Word: rapture

True definition: a state of overwhelming excitement

My definition: covering a present

Sentence: "He said, 'So what if I *rapture* gift in newspaper? It's the gift that counts!'"

Word: ratios

True definition: differences of data, length, or growth

My definition: a debt owed to Ray

Sentence: "It's *ratios* the money to and not me!"

Word: rebate

True definition: to return a part of a payment or purchase

My definition: fishing action

Sentence: "That fish just took the worm off my hook, so I have to *rebate* my pole!"

Word: rectifier

True definition: a device that converts AC current to DC current

My definition: a terrible firefighter driver

Sentence: "They banned the rookie from driving because he *rectifier* truck twice!"

Smittionary
"Not your ordinary dictionary"
To get the best effect, say the italicized word(s) slowly

Word: rectum

True definition: a part of the intestine that digests food

My definition: a terrible firefighter driver

Sentence: "The rookie firefighter also has two cars at home, and he *rectum* both!"

Word: redefine

True definition: to take another look with a purpose to change or alter

My definition: hasty decision aversion

Sentence: "The next time I sign something, I'll be sure to *redefine* print first!"

Word: redesign

True definition: to alter or change the look of something

My definition: posted rules

Sentence: "'No loitering' is what it says if you *redesign* correctly!"

Word: redistribute

True definition: to spread to other areas

My definition: showing admiration

Sentence: "Don't talk to me while I *redistribute* to this great singer!"

Smittionary
"Not your ordinary dictionary"
To get the best effect, say the italicized word(s) slowly

Word: reefer

True definition: another word for *marijuana*

My definition: a round holiday decoration

Sentence: "I think I need a new Christmas *reefer* my front door!"

Word: reindeer

True definition: Santa's animals

My definition: bad-weather warning

Sentence: "You'd better take your umbrella because it looks like it's going to *reindeer!*"

Word: require

True definition: to ask for a need or want

My definition: replacement group singers

Sentence: "All the singers quit, so the pastor had to *require* his church with new singers."

Word: requisite

True definition: something essential or necessary

My definition: trying to recall an accident

Sentence: "Which *requisite* that you didn't have on your seat belt?"

Smittionary
"Not your ordinary dictionary"
To get the best effect, say the italicized word(s) slowly

Word: ricotta

True definition: Italian cheese

My definition: advice for Rick

Sentence: "I think *ricotta* sue the people that hit him with the car!"

Word: ringmaster

True definition: one in charge of circus performances

My definition: temporary blindness

Sentence: "The brightness of that three-carat *ringmaster* vision up for three days!"

Word: rinse

True definition: to flush or soak with water

My definition: paying to use something temporarily

Sentence: "I will help to drive if he *rinse* the car for the weekend!"

Word: rocketry

True definition: the study and experimentation of rockets

My definition: strong wind action

Sentence: "These storms we had lately were strong enough to *rocketry* back and forth!"

Smittionary
"Not your ordinary dictionary"
To get the best effect, say the italicized word(s) slowly

Word: roulette

True definition: gambling game using a ball and a spinning wheel

My definition: wearing the pants

Sentence: "Joe's wife said, 'He may think he makes decisions, but I *roulette* house over there!'"

Word: rubberize

True definition: to coat with rubber

My definition: wiping away tears

Sentence: "Tell her not to *rubberize* because they will be red and irritated!"

Word: rugby

True definition: English football-type sport

My definition: carpet

Sentence: "Watch your step because my new *rugby* tripping people coming in the door!"

Word: rummy

True definition: a card game

My definition: needing a ride somewhere

Sentence: "Hey, man, can you *rummy* to the store?"

Smittionary
"Not your ordinary dictionary"
To get the best effect, say the italicized word(s) slowly

Word: Russia

True definition: a country

My definition: in a hurry

Sentence: "I don't mean to *Russia*, but I have to be at work in ten minutes!"

Word: Russian

True definition: a native of Russia

My definition: hurrying

Sentence: "He must be late for work again because he is *Russian* everybody!"

Smittionary
"Not your ordinary dictionary"
To get the best effect, say the italicized word(s) slowly

S

Word: Saginaw
True definition: a city in Michigan
My definition: a bad fashion statement
Sentence: "I hate seeing people with their pants *Saginaw* down to their thighs!"

Word: Sagittarian
True definition: a member of the zodiac sign
My definition: destroying
Sentence: "It's so *Sagittarian* up the new shoes I just bought you!"

Word: Samoa
True definition: an island
My definition: extra helping
Sentence: "Can I have *Samoa* potatoes please?"

Smittionary
"Not your ordinary dictionary"
To get the best effect, say the italicized word(s) slowly

Word: San Bernardino's
True definition: a California city's claim
My definition: a hurt Flintstone's pet
Sentence: "Fred Wilma and Pebbles had to leave
the beach because the *San Bernardino's* feet!"

Word: sanctifier
True definition: Holy Spirit
My definition: underwater
Sentence: "The fire chief was mad at the new
recruit because he *sanctifier* truck in the
river!"

Word: San Diego
True definition: a city in California
My definition: a breakfast food choice
Sentence: "After testing other waffles, he keeps
San Diego waffles taste the best!"

Word: Sarasota
True definition: a city in Florida
My definition: a salesperson
Sentence: "This week alone, *Sarasota* TV,
microwave, and three DVD players!"

Word: Saskatchewan
True definition: a Canadian province

Smittionary
"Not your ordinary dictionary"
To get the best effect, say the italicized word(s) slowly

My definition: learning how to fish

Sentence: "Pa says you know how to fish now, and he *Saskatchewan* like he showed you!"

Word: satiate

True definition: to satisfy as a need

My definition: food consumption

Sentence: "Margaret *satiate* only one brownie, but three were missing!"

Word: satin

True definition: a silklike material

My definition: trickery

Sentence: "Don't move those papers. I think someone is *satin* you up!"

Word: satire

True definition: a type of humor or act

My definition: tire change instruction

Sentence: "To lift the car, you have to *satire* jack under the car first!"

Word: saturate

True definition: to soak or fill something usually with liquid

My definition: interest measurement

Smittionary
"Not your ordinary dictionary"
To get the best effect, say the italicized word(s) slowly

Sentence: "Since he can't afford 14 percent interest, you can *saturate* a little lower to make the sale!"

Word: sawyer
True definition: a type of Japanese beetle
My definition: spotting someone
Sentence: "I *sawyer* sister at the mall earlier today!"

Word: scab
True definition: hardened blood on a cut or sore
My definition: transportation
Sentence: "I hope this *scab* driver knows where he is going!"

Word: scald
True definition: to burn badly usually with liquid
My definition: a title
Sentence: "I read a great book last month, but I forgot what it *scald*!"

Word: scepter
True definition: a staff or baton used as an emblem of authority

Smittionary
"Not your ordinary dictionary"
To get the best effect, say the italicized word(s) slowly

My definition: left out

Sentence: "Poor Mary! Everyone *scepter* got to go on the field trip last week!"

Word: scholar

True definition: an enrolled student or pupil

My definition: foldable top part of a shirt or jacket

Sentence: "She got mad at him because he had lipstick on his *scholar*!"

Word: scintillate

True definition: to emit or produce sparks

My definition: not meeting a deadline

Sentence: "She will not get credit for the class because her final paper was *scintillate*!"

Word: scooter

True definition: a skateboard-like riding toy

My definition: pushed over

Sentence: "Mary jumped up and punched Jimmy because he *scooter* off her chair!"

Word: scrimp

True definition: a smaller-than-normal portion or stinginess

My definition: seafood item

Smittionary
"Not your ordinary dictionary"
To get the best effect, say the italicized word(s) slowly

Sentence: "I went to a seafood place and ordered *scrimp* scampi!"

Word: scripter
True definition: one who writes a screenplay
My definition: taking something away
Sentence: "After they found indecent pictures of the pageant winner, they *scripter* of her crown!"

Word: scubas
True definition: people who dive underwater with breathing equipment
My definition: school transportation
Sentence: "He was late for school again because he missed the *scubas*!"

Word: scurry
True definition: to move about in a fast pace
My definition: frightening
Sentence: "I've had nightmares ever since I watched that *scurry* movie!"

Word: sea otter
True definition: a brown animal that stays near water
My definition: a breakup line

Smittionary
"Not your ordinary dictionary"
To get the best effect, say the italicized word(s) slowly

Sentence: "We gave it another try, but I think we should *sea otter* people!"

Word: secondary
True definition: not first in order of importance
My definition: bad dairy food
Sentence: "I told the manager that this was the *secondary* item I purchased that was spoiled!"

Word: selfish
True definition: not willing to share
My definition: seafood business
Sentence: "My cousin opened a seafood store so he could *selfish* for a living!"

Word: semicircle
True definition: half of a circle
My definition: a kid proud of his drawing skills
Sentence: "Hey, mom! Come and *semicircle* I drew!"

Word: senate
True definition: legislative assembly
My definition: eyewitness

Smittionary
"Not your ordinary dictionary"
To get the best effect, say the italicized word(s) slowly

Sentence: "Yes, he robbed that lady! I *senate* with my own eyes!"

Word: senior
True definition: an older person or a student at the top grade level
My definition: spotted
Sentence: "I *senior* car at the mall yesterday!"

Word: sensibilia
True definition: something that may be sensed
My definition: an accounting mistake
Sentence: "Mr. Smith, I will send you a full refund *sensibilia* twice for your purchase!"

Word: September
True definition: ninth month of the year
My definition: forgotten tree-cutter warning
Sentence: "The lumberjack yelled everything *September* when the tree he cut was falling!"

Word: sediment
True definition: residue settled on the bottom of liquid
My definition: nonworking breath aid

Smittionary
"Not your ordinary dictionary"
To get the best effect, say the italicized word(s) slowly

Sentence: "She *sediment* didn't help him because his breath still stank!"

Word: seizure
True definition: uncontrollable convulsions
My definition: to view
Sentence: "James says he *seizure* mom at bingo every Saturday!"

Word: seldom
True definition: rare occurrence
My definition: money waste
Sentence: "A good con artist can *seldom* people anything!"

Word: semicolon
True definition: a punctuation mark
My definition: seeing your insides
Sentence: "After the x-rays, the doctor let me *semicolon* was cleaned out good!"

Word: Serbia
True definition: a country
My definition: alcoholic beverage distribution
Sentence: "Do they still *Serbia* and wine at the restaurant?"

Smittionary
"Not your ordinary dictionary"
To get the best effect, say the italicized word(s) slowly

Word: sewer

True definition: a waste drainage system

My definition: taking someone to court for damages

Sentence: "Since she slandered your name, you can *sewer* for damages!"

Word: Seymour

True definition: a first or last name

My definition: better vision

Sentence: "He wanted a window seat so he could *Seymour* sights on the trip!"

Word: shadow

True definition: an image of someone or something depending on light position

My definition: timid or quiet

Sentence: "I thought she was *shadow* others said she really wasn't!"

Word: Shakespeare

True definition: a poet

My definition: prehistoric defense mechanism

Sentence: "If saber-toothed tiger growl, just *Shakespeare* at him, and he will run away!"

Smittionary
"Not your ordinary dictionary"
To get the best effect, say the italicized word(s) slowly

Word: Shannon
True definition: a female name
My definition: stinginess
Sentence: "He ate that whole pie and didn't *Shannon* with the rest of us!"

Word: Sharon
True definition: a female name
My definition: giving to others
Sentence: "He felt bad about the pie, so next time, he will be *Sharon* it with us!"

Word: shellac
True definition: a liquid wood-finishing gloss
My definition: fond of
Sentence: "From the way she was staring at me, I think *shellac* me!"

Word: sheriff
True definition: law officer
My definition: approval
Sentence: "Can I go to the game with you? *Sheriff* it's okay with your parents!"

Word: shoulder
True definition: body part between the arm socket and neck

Smittionary
"Not your ordinary dictionary"
To get the best effect, say the italicized word(s) slowly

My definition: visual instruction

Sentence: "She didn't understand instructions, so I *shoulder* how to nail the boards together!"

Word: shudder

True definition: to shake or tremble

My definition: to close

Sentence: "A gentleman will always open and *shudder* car door for her when she leaves!"

Word: shut-eye

True definition: slang for sleep

My definition: wishy-washy decision

Sentence: "There's a party tonight. So *shut-eye* go, or *shut-eye* stay home?"

Word: sideburns

True definition: hair on both sides of a man's face

My definition: exercise results

Sentence: "My whole left *sideburns* from the Zumba class today!"

Word: sienna

True definition: an earthly substance that is used in pigment

Smittionary
"Not your ordinary dictionary"
To get the best effect, say the italicized word(s) slowly

My definition: Peeping Tom diversion

Sentence: "Her mother told her to close her curtains so no one can *sienna* window!"

Word: siesta

True definition: a noontime nap usually in Mexico

My definition: a funny TV-show character

Sentence: "I always loved to *siesta* call her brother-in-law a fish-eyed fool!"

Word: silicon

True definition: a material used in sealants on electronics

My definition: a dumb inmate

Sentence: "Did you know that *silicon* tried to break out of prison again?"

Word: sinuosity

True definition: being wavy or winding in nature

My definition: visitors' guide forwarding

Sentence: "The travel agent will *sinuosity* map so you can find our local attractions easily!"

Word: sinus

True definition: part of the nostril that contains air movement

Smittionary
"Not your ordinary dictionary"
To get the best effect, say the italicized word(s) slowly

My definition: a contract agreement

Sentence: "We were so fed up with satellite that I went to *sinus* up for cable!"

Word: Sioux Falls

True definition: a city in South Dakota

My definition: your friend tumbling

Sentence: "I swear, the next time *Sioux Falls* in the water, I'm laughing!"

Word: Sirius

True definition: a bright star of the constellation

My definition: not joking

Sentence: "He said I owed back taxes, and I asked him if he was *Sirius*."

Word: sitcom

True definition: a TV show with humor

My definition: relaxed

Sentence: "I told the boys to please *sitcom* while I go vote!"

Word: sixmo

True definition: the size of a piece of paper cut six from a sheet

My definition: an amount

Smittionary
"Not your ordinary dictionary"
To get the best effect, say the italicized word(s) slowly

Sentence: "He was hungry because after he ate the first six wings, he ordered *sixmo*!"

Word: skidder
True definition: a truck used for hauling logs
My definition: slang for completing something
Sentence: "We have a lot of work ahead of us, so let's *skidder* done!"

Word: skillet
True definition: a frying pan
My definition: ending a life
Sentence: "There's a snake in the backyard, so let *skillet* before it bites someone!"

Word: skimobile
True definition: motorized vehicle for driving on snow
My definition: a winter activity compliment to your friend Bill
Sentence: "You really should *skimobile*! You did a great job on the slopes!"

Word: skinny
True definition: a person that's very thin
My definition: leg abrasion

Smittionary
"Not your ordinary dictionary"
To get the best effect, say the italicized word(s) slowly

Sentence: "He said he fell down and happened to *skinny* on the sidewalk!"

Word: skirmish
True definition: a mild fight or debate'
My definition: frightening someone
Sentence: "You boys should be ashamed! Y'all done *skirmish* Susie to death with that snake!"

Word: s'more
True definition: a dessert with graham crackers, marshmallows, and chocolate
My definition: additional
Sentence: "Your son is really hungry because he just asked for *s'more* potatoes and carrots!"

Word: smother
True definition: to suffocate or to be right under someone
My definition: additional
Sentence: "The bus cannot leave because we are waiting on *smother* people to board!"

Word: sneaker
True definition: a tennis shoe

Smittionary
"Not your ordinary dictionary"
To get the best effect, say the italicized word(s) slowly

My definition: discreet entrance

Sentence: "He got caught trying to *sneaker* in his window last night!"

Word: snit

True definition: a state of agitation

My definition: clothing material

Sentence: "I thought this shirt was polyester but found out it *snit*!"

Word: snow cone

True definition: ice formed into a ball with flavoring

My definition: food trickery

Sentence: "Hey! This *snow cone* bread! It tastes like cake instead!"

Word: snooker

True definition: a type of billiards or pool game

My definition: discreet exit

Sentence: "His father was in the living room, so he *snooker* out of his bedroom window."

Word: snot

True definition: nasal mucous

My definition: isn't

Smittionary
"Not your ordinary dictionary"
To get the best effect, say the italicized word(s) slowly

Sentence: "After her weird sneeze, she told everyone that it *snot* funny!"

Word: snuff
True definition: to put out a candle flame
My definition: sufficient amount
Sentence: "Okay, that's *snuff* playing for today!"

Word: soccer
True definition: a sport where hands and arms cannot be used
My definition: to punch
Sentence: "He really didn't mean to *soccer* in the eye with the ball!"

Word: soda
True definition: another name for a soft drink
My definition: offered for purchase
Sentence: "Joe *soda* whopping ten-thousand worth of appliances last month!"

Word: sodium
True definition: an alkali ingredient found in food and drinks
My definition: salesman activity

Smittionary
"Not your ordinary dictionary"
To get the best effect, say the italicized word(s) slowly

Sentence: "Isn't that the guy that *sodium* their new car yesterday?"

Word: sodium nitrate
True definition: a crystallized salt used for fertilizer
My definition: a better hotel rate
Sentence: "Since it was after 3:00 p.m., he *sodium nitrate* on the hotel room!"

Word: soldier
True definition: a person in the military
My definition: give away for money
Sentence: "I hope you don't mind that I *soldier* stamp collection yesterday!"

Word: solo
True definition: music performed by one person
My definition: almost quiet
Sentence: "He talks *solo* that we can barely hear him!"

Word: Somerset
True definition: a city in Kentucky
My definition: state of mind
Sentence: "You have to be patient with old people because *Somerset* in their ways!"

Smittionary
"Not your ordinary dictionary"
To get the best effect, say the italicized word(s) slowly

Word: sonogram

True definition: a picture taken of the inside
of someone

My definition: drug-dealer mistake

Sentence: "I had him arrested for trying to
sell my *sonogram* of cocaine!"

Word: soupy

True definition: foggy or cloudy

My definition: your friend Sue's embarrassment

Sentence: "She was so drunk I literally saw
soupy on herself!"

Word: sparrow

True definition: a small bird

My definition: extra

Sentence: "I usually keep a *sparrow* of toilet
tissue in the bathroom!"

Word: spirit

True definition: the inner quality or nature of
a person

My definition: one way to kill an animal

Sentence: "The caveman couldn't kill the
tiger with rocks, so he decided to *spirit*!"

Smittionary
"Not your ordinary dictionary"
To get the best effect, say the italicized word(s) slowly

Word: stadium

True definition: an arena for sports or concerts

My definition: not bright

Sentence: "Instead of bringing the lights up, let them *stadium* until the end of the play!"

Word: stairwell

True definition: a place in a building where stairs are located

My definition: to mix thoroughly

Sentence: "The instructions say to pour in the ingredients and *stairwell* for five minutes!"

Word: stanza

True definition: a group of lines in a poem

My definition: Stan accolades

Sentence: "Everyone here knows that *Stanza* great guy to work with!"

Word: stardom

True definition: the state of being a very famous performer

My definition: to begin

Sentence: "For the new employees, he said to *stardom* out at minimum wage!"

Smittionary
"Not your ordinary dictionary"
To get the best effect, say the italicized word(s) slowly

Word: steelmaker

True definition: a manufacturer of steel

My definition: smitten

Sentence: "Just his presence can *steelmaker* heart skip a beat!"

Word: steelworker

True definition: a steelworker business employee

My definition: negative effect

Sentence: "His arrogance and attitude can *steelworker* last nerve!"

Word: stepfather

True definition: a nonbiological male parent

My definition: more distance

Sentence: "With his size-14 shoe, he was able to *stepfather* than his brother."

Word: stereo

True definition: sound produced with a left and right channel

My definition: cooking tip

Sentence: "When cooking rice, be sure to *stereo* slow so it won't stick."

Word: sternum

True definition: a bone that connects the ribs

Smittionary
"Not your ordinary dictionary"
To get the best effect, say the italicized word(s) slowly

My definition: cooking action

Sentence: "These potatoes still have lumps, and I'm *sternum* as fast as I can!"

Word: Steuben

True definition: a Prussian-born American military general

My definition: inquiring about your friend Stewart

Sentence: "I wonder what *Steuben* up to lately!"

Word: stigma

True definition: a mark of shame or discredit

My definition: forceful entry

Sentence: "Will you get mad if I *stigma* tongue out at you?"

Word: stigmatize

True definition: to describe or identify in disgraceful terms

My definition: placement of a suit accessory

Sentence: "I think I will *stigmatize* in here with my suits!"

Word: stiletto

True definition: a pointed instrument for piercing holes for eyelets

Smittionary
"Not your ordinary dictionary"
To get the best effect, say the italicized word(s) slowly

My definition: no thieving intentions

Sentence: "Ain't nobody trying to *stiletto* piece of junk car of yours!"

Word: stirrup

True definition: horse-mounting aides

My definition: cause or create

Sentence: "Watch them because they always like to *stirrup* trouble!"

Word: stool pigeon

True definition: a person acting as a decoy or informer

My definition: throwing of seats

Sentence: "That was some bar fight! I've never seen so much *stool pigeon* in all my days!"

Word: stranger

True definition: someone unknown

My definition: to drain liquid from

Sentence: "You should have *stranger* peas after boiling them to prevent sogginess!"

Word: stupor

True definition: a state of extreme apathy from shock

My definition: food rationing

Smittionary
"Not your ordinary dictionary"
To get the best effect, say the italicized word(s) slowly

Sentence: "Tell the people that there is only one bowl of *stupor* person!"

Word: stylobate
True definition: a continuous flat coping or pavement supporting a row of architectural columns
My definition: type of fishing lure
Sentence: "He was using the wrong *stylobate* for his rod and reel!"

Word: stylus
True definition: an instrument for writing
My definition: dressing with the latest trends
Sentence: "We let the fashion guru *stylus* for the new millennium!"

Word: subjugator
True definition: one who controls others
My definition: a material switch
Sentence: "We didn't have them in stock so we *subjugator* boots with snakeskin ones!"

Word: substitute
True definition: to take the place of
My definition: horn blowing on an underwater craft

Smittionary
"Not your ordinary dictionary"
To get the best effect, say the italicized word(s) slowly

Sentence: "George tried to get the navy *substitute* their battle-sound horns!"

Word: subulate
True definition: linear and tapering to a fine point
My definition: a tardy student when regular teacher is off
Sentence: "I am going to have to tell the *subulate* for class again!"

Word: suffocate
True definition: to deprive of oxygen
My definition: Kate's dilemma
Sentence: "I know it's rough, but you don't have to *suffocate*!"

Word: summarize
True definition: to tell in or reduce to a summary
My definition: garden problems
Sentence: "The thing about crops is that *summarize* and some will not!"

Word: summer
True definition: one of the four seasons
My definition: distinguishing

Smittionary
"Not your ordinary dictionary"
To get the best effect, say the italicized word(s) slowly

Sentence: "These kids! *Summer* real good, and some are bad!"

Word: sunroof
True definition: an automobile panel that can open and close
My definition: your offspring working
Sentence: "I stood proudly and watched my *sunroof* his house!"

Word: sunstruck
True definition: affected or touched by the sun
My definition: not getting a hit
Sentence: "I can't believe that my *sunstruck* out four times today!"

Word: Super Bowl
True definition: the NFL final championship game
My definition: food rationing
Sentence: "Due to the shortage, they are only giving out two ladles of *Super Bowl* today!"

Word: sure
True definition: firmly established

Smittionary
"Not your ordinary dictionary"
To get the best effect, say the italicized word(s) slowly

My definition: to outfit a horse's foot

Sentence: "She paid me good money to *sure* horse!"

Word: sycamore

True definition: a type of tree

My definition: dog attack

Sentence: "I thought he would *sycamore* vicious dog on me than a poodle!"

Word: synthesize

True definition: to combine music parts to produce a whole sound

My definition: to forward fitting information

Sentence: "The seamstress was patient while the bride *synthesize* of her dress to her!"

Smittionary
"Not your ordinary dictionary"
To get the best effect, say the italicized word(s) slowly

T

Word: Taiwan
True definition: a part of China
My definition: twisting action
    for a neat result
Sentence: "I love the neckties,
    but I haven't learned how to *Taiwan* yet!"

Word: tamale
True definition: Mexican food wrapped in
    dough
My definition: delivery to Molly
Sentence: "Can you please take these forms
    tamale for me? She needs them ASAP!"

Word: tampon
True definition: a feminine hygiene product
My definition: to step on
Sentence: "I told him to take his foot and
    tampon the fire!"

Smittionary
"Not your ordinary dictionary"
To get the best effect, say the italicized word(s) slowly

Word: Tanaka

True definition: a Japanese surname

My definition: striking someone unconscious

Sentence: "If they keep messing with me, I'm
going *Tanaka* person out cold!"

Word: tandem

True definition: working or occurring in con-
junction with each other

My definition: darkening by the sun

Sentence: "They just got back from Florida,
and the sun *tandem* pretty good!"

Word: target

True definition: a mark to shoot at or for

My definition: a vehicle's rubber-wheel surface

Sentence: "That light comes on to warn you
when your *target* too low on air!"

Word: tartar

True definition: an incrustation on the teeth
consisting of plaque

My definition: helping someone learn

Sentence: "My little girl is so happy that I *tartar* how to count to ten!"

Smittionary
"Not your ordinary dictionary"
To get the best effect, say the italicized word(s) slowly

Word: tattoo

True definition: to mark or color the skin with ink

My definition: to twist in a knot or bow shape

Sentence: "The criminal had to *tattoo* of them together to save time and rope!"

Word: taxonomist

True definition: a person who studies the natural relationships of plants and animals

My definition: a terrible statistics recorder

Sentence: "Along with three missed shots, the scorekeeper *taxonomist* free throw by the superstar!"

Word: Taylor

True definition: someone's first or last name

My definition: to inform

Sentence: "I just don't have the heart to *Taylor* she didn't get the part!"

Word: teaser

True definition: one that makes fun of

My definition: a golf action

Sentence: "He notices her form as she *teaser* first shot!"

Smittionary
"Not your ordinary dictionary"
To get the best effect, say the italicized word(s) slowly

Word: techno
True definition: a type of dance music
My definition: not accepting
Sentence: "My father is tough because he don't *techno* crap off of anyone!"

Word: technophile
True definition: an enthusiast of technology
My definition: falsely accused
Sentence: "I told you that I didn't *technophile* from that file cabinet!"

Word: technophobias
True definition: fears or dislikes of advanced technology or complex devices
My definition: a drinking bet
Sentence: "I told you it wouldn't *technophobias* to get him drunk!"

Word: telecom
True definition: short for *telecommunication technology*
My definition: dealing with peaceful people
Sentence: "I love it when I have to *telecom* person some bad news!"

Smittionary
"Not your ordinary dictionary"
To get the best effect, say the italicized word(s) slowly

Word: telegram
True definition: an electronically sent message or greeting
My definition: drug recognition
Sentence: "I am from the streets, and I can *telegram* of cocaine from flour when I see it!"

Word: telephony
True definition: the use of an apparatus for transmission of sounds between points
My definition: spotting a fake
Sentence: "I can *telephony* person from a real, sincere one!"

Word: telephotos
True definition: pictures made larger photographed from a distance
My definition: doctor's foot diagnosis
Sentence: "Nurse, when you see Mrs. Johnson, *telephotos* can be saved out of five on her left foot!"

Word: telescope
True definition: an instrument used to view faraway objects
My definition: mouthwash advice for a woman

Smittionary
"Not your ordinary dictionary"
To get the best effect, say the italicized word(s) slowly

Sentence: "The dentist made sure to *telescope* helps with halitosis!"

Word: telluride
True definition: a binary compound of tellurium with a more electropositive element or group
My definition: the person designated to drive
Sentence: "You need to *telluride* they have to wait until you change clothes, young lady!"

Word: tenacity
True definition: the state of being persistent in maintaining or seeking something valued or desired
My definition: a joke
Sentence: "If only five people lived in a city, it could be called a *tenacity*!"

Word: Tennessee
True definition: a state
My definition: teacher's grades
Sentence: "Out of twenty-five students, the teacher gave five an A, ten a B, and *Tennessee*!"

Smittionary
"Not your ordinary dictionary"
To get the best effect, say the italicized word(s) slowly

Word: tequila

True definition: Mexican liquor distilled from the fermented sap of an agave

My definition: commit murder

Sentence: "Most gangs require their new recruits *tequila* random person!"

Word: terrible

True definition: extremely bad

My definition: very hungry

Sentence: "I have seen some hungry people *terrible* of soup up!"

Word: terrorist

True definition: a person that uses terror for coercion

My definition: an arm-part accident

Sentence: "The machine began to *terrorist* from her arm, but they shut it down in time!"

Word: testament

True definition: an expression of conviction

My definition: breath aid

Sentence: "The company decided to *testament* they invented on the person with the worst breath!"

Smittionary
"Not your ordinary dictionary"
To get the best effect, say the italicized word(s) slowly

Word: testifier

True definition: a person who gives evidence

My definition: pyromaniac

Sentence: "The crazy person always has to *testifier* to see if it really burns!"

Word: testimony

True definition: a firsthand authentication of a fact

My definition: a currency examiner

Sentence: "I would love to be the person to *testimony* for defects at the Federal Reserve!"

Word: thatcher

True definition: a machine that covers with plant material such as straw

My definition: recognition

Sentence: "Hey, isn't *thatcher* grandma out there flashing people?"

Word: therapist

True definition: a person trained in methods of nondrug rehabilitation

My definition: an upset urine-sample response

Sentence: "*Therapist*! Are you happy now, nurse?"

Smittionary
"Not your ordinary dictionary"
To get the best effect, say the italicized word(s) slowly

Word: therefore
True definition: on that grounds or for that
    reason
My definition: the age of kids
Sentence: "How old are my twins? *Therefore*
    years old!"

Word: thereto
True definition: meaning to that
My definition: other kids' ages
Sentence: "My brother has a set of twins also.
    and *thereto* years old!"

Word: thermometry
True definition: measurement of temperature
My definition: a large plant gift
Sentence: "The thoughtful kids planted *ther-
    mometry* for her birthday this year!"

Word: thermos
True definition: a vacuum container for keep-
    ing food or liquids hot or cold
My definition: finding fault
Sentence: "I only bought two items, and you
    charged me for three! *Thermos* be some
    mistake!"

Smittionary
"Not your ordinary dictionary"
To get the best effect, say the italicized word(s) slowly

Word: thespian

True definition: of or relating to Thespis, the Greek poet

My definition: urinating

Sentence: "Come and get your kids! *Thespian* in the pool again!"

Word: thingamabob

True definition: something that is hard to name or describe

My definition: a difficult handless game

Sentence: "I have strong teeth, so I *thingamabob* for apples in the next contest!"

Word: thrice

True definition: three times

My definition: wedding tradition

Sentence: "Everyone threw *thrice* at the couple as they left the church!"

Word: throng

True definition: a multitude of assembled persons

My definition: mistaken identity

Sentence: "I hate to tell you this, but you have *throng* guy in custody!"

Word: thrum

Smittionary
"Not your ordinary dictionary"
To get the best effect, say the italicized word(s) slowly

True definition: a tuft or short piece of rope yarn used in canvas

My definition: alcoholic beverage

Sentence: "I usually can handle my liquor, but *thrum* was potent in this bar!"

Word: thrush

True definition: a disease that is caused by a fungus

My definition: a hurried action

Sentence: "I usually take my break early, and my boss asked me what's *thrush*!"

Word: thrust

True definition: to put forcibly into a course of action

My definition: metal reaction with moisture

Sentence: "I was going to buy that car, but *thrust* was too bad on it!"

Word: Thursday

True definition: a day of the week

My definition: a hotel reservation

Sentence: "Since they had trouble with the room, *Thursday* has been extended two more days free of charge!"

Smittionary
"Not your ordinary dictionary"
To get the best effect, say the italicized word(s) slowly

Word: thwack

True definition: a heavy blow or strike and the sound

My definition: lame

Sentence: "We were bored, so we left *thwack* party!"

Word: thylacines

True definition: Tasmanian tigers

My definition: the symbols over the number 4 on a computer keyboard ($).

Sentence: "He married the rich girl because he saw *thylacines* in his future!"

Word: toboggan

True definition: a type of hat

My definition: trying to get a lower price

Sentence: "Some people only go to yard sales *toboggan* with the sellers!"

Word: token

True definition: a coin-like piece used in place of money

My definition: foot part

Sentence: "A bad *token* ruin your running ability!"

Smittionary
"Not your ordinary dictionary"
To get the best effect, say the italicized word(s) slowly

Word: Tokyo
True definition: the capital of Japan
My definition: to scratch
Sentence: "She was so mad at you that she
was going *Tokyo* car last night!"

Word: tomahawk
True definition: an Indian weapon
My definition: a bird gift
Sentence: "Those crazy in-laws bought *toma-
hawk* for his birthday!"

Word: tomorrow
True definition: the day after today
My definition: a specified area
Sentence: "I am going to tend *tomorrow* of
corn and green beans I planted last week!"

Word: Topeka
True definition: the capital of Kansas
My definition: a baby-and-adult game
Sentence: "My little toddler loves *Topeka* boo
with everyone she sees!"

Word: toponym
True definition: a name of a place or the location of the thing named

Smittionary
"Not your ordinary dictionary"
To get the best effect, say the italicized word(s) slowly

My definition: over or on

Sentence: "They were lucky because that tree almost fell on *toponym*!"

Word: Torino

True definition: a car made by Ford

My definition: a vacation spot in Nevada

Sentence: "We decided to go *Torino* for our vacation this year!"

Word: torso

True definition: a sculptured representation of the trunk of a human body

My definition: ripped or cut

Sentence: "The paper was wet, and that's why it *torso* easily!"

Word: tortoise

True definition: any of a family of turtles

My definition: to show how

Sentence: "My dad got us bicycles and *tortoise* how to ride them!"

Word: torture

True definition: the infliction of intense pain

My definition: to set fire to

Smittionary
"Not your ordinary dictionary"
To get the best effect, say the italicized word(s) slowly

Sentence: "Even though it's a piece of junk, that's no reason to *torture* car for insurance purposes!"

Word: totalist
True definition: of or relating to the aims of the music of totalism
My definition: to rip or tear up
Sentence: "I forgot who was scheduled today because my dog *totalist* up with the names!"

Word: totem
True definition: a family or clan identified by a common totemic object such as a pole
My definition: to inform
Sentence: "I *totem* four times not to go into that old house!"

Word: toucan
True definition: a tropical bird with brilliant colors
My definition: more than one but less than three
Sentence: "Since he is such a smart aleck, *toucan* play that game!"

Smittionary
"Not your ordinary dictionary"
To get the best effect, say the italicized word(s) slowly

Word: touchable

True definition: allowing yourself or something to be felt or affected

My definition: handling of a soup dish

Sentence: "Remember, if you *touchable*, you must wash it afterward!"

Word: touché

True definition: the success of an argument, accusation, or a witty point

My definition: gifting an heiress

Sentence: "His will reads, 'And *touch*é, I leave my stamp collection!'"

Word: toupee

True definition: a wig section of hair that covers a bald spot

My definition: collection for services

Sentence: "I am getting ready *toupee* for my hair extensions!"

Word: Tourette's

True definition: a neurological disorder with involuntary body movements

My definition: rodents

Smittionary
"Not your ordinary dictionary"
To get the best effect, say the italicized word(s) slowly

Sentence: "While walking in the alley, I saw *Tourette's* running inside an abandoned building!"

Word: touring
True definition: participating in a journey or trip
My definition: doorbell action
Sentence: "I am going *touring* that doorbell one more time, and then I'm going to knock on the door!"

Word: tournament
True definition: a series of games to determine a champion team or individual
My definition: bad-breath statement
Sentence: "His breath is so bad he can *tournament* into fire!"

Word: towplane
True definition: an airplane that tows gliders for flight
My definition: foot part
Sentence: "I can't believe she polished nine toes and left one *towplane*!"

Smittionary
"Not your ordinary dictionary"
To get the best effect, say the italicized word(s) slowly

Word: Toyama

True definition: a city in Japan

My definition: to inform their mother

Sentence: "I went back and *Toyama* that you are going with us!"

Word: Toyota

True definition: a car company and a city in Japan

My definition: a *Star Wars* figure

Sentence: "I love *Star Wars*, so my mom bought me a *Toyota* doll for my birthday!"

Word: trabeate

True definition: to design or construct with horizontal beams or lintels

My definition: Trey's age

Sentence: "I was wondering, will *trabeate* or nine on his birthday?"

Word: tracing

True definition: the act of copying something on its lines

My definition: Trey's musical talent

Sentence: "If you have the chance to hear *tracing*, you are in for a treat!"

Smittionary
"Not your ordinary dictionary"
To get the best effect, say the italicized word(s) slowly

Word: tragedy

True definition: a disastrous event

My definition: attempt at the opposite team play from the offense

Sentence: "The coach said, 'I *tragedy*, but my offense ran through it too easily!'"

Word: trampoline

True definition: an apparatus used to jump on, flip, or pounce on

My definition: making fun of a harlot

Sentence: "He jokingly called that *trampoline* mean, fighting machine!"

Word: treasonous

True definition: able to commit treason

My definition: large plants with branches and leaves

Sentence: "The strong wind blew three *treasonous*, but no one got hurt!"

Word: triable

True definition: liable or subject to judicial examination or trial

My definition: sampling food

Sentence: "You really ought to *triable* of this soup! It is very good!"

Smittionary
"Not your ordinary dictionary"
To get the best effect, say the italicized word(s) slowly

Word: triarchy

True definition: government by three persons

My definition: offering of an unlocking device

Sentence: "Since your key didn't work, you are welcome to *triarchy* next!"

Word: trigonometry

True definition: the study of the properties of triangles

My definition: Roy Roger's horse blamed for eating roots

Sentence: "My apples stopped growing because my horse *trigonometry* roots out of the ground!"

Word: trimester

True definition: a period of three or about three months

My definition: bad attempt

Sentence: "She should've quit after the second time because that third *trimester* score up!"

Word: trinomial

True definition: consisting of three mathematical terms

My definition: restaurant-food avoidance

Smittionary
"Not your ordinary dictionary"
To get the best effect, say the italicized word(s) slowly

Sentence: "Since the restaurant has bad reviews, I will *trinomial* prepared there!"

Word: truculent
True definition: feeling or displaying ferocity or cruelty
My definition: a vehicle loan
Sentence: "Do you remember that *truculent* your neighbor? Well, he totaled it!"

Word: tuba
True definition: a low-pitched musical instrument
My definition: a container
Sentence: "He went through a *tuba* toothpaste in four days!"

Word: tubeless
True definition: a tire that has no inner tube
My definition: grace before a meal
Sentence: "We are ready to eat! Who is going *tubeless* the food?"

Word: tuckahoe
True definition: an Indian food
My definition: stealing a garden tool

Smittionary
"Not your ordinary dictionary"
To get the best effect, say the italicized word(s) slowly

Sentence: "The poor farmer tried to *tucka-hoe* in his coat and walk out of the store without paying for it!"

Word: Tuesday
True definition: a day of the week
My definition: not moving or going
Sentence: "Are you really going *Tuesday* the entire week with us?"

Word: tuition
True definition: the price of or payment for instruction
My definition: a front-leg part
Sentence: "He suffered a nasty blow *tuition* bone and will be out for three weeks!"

Word: tulips
True definition: flowers
My definition: mouth parts
Sentence: "Most people have *tulips*! I haven't seen anybody with just one!"

Word: tumor
True definition: a swollen or distended part
My definition: additional

Smittionary
"Not your ordinary dictionary"
To get the best effect, say the italicized word(s) slowly

Sentence: "He liked the sausages so much he
ordered *tumor* to go!"

Word: Tupelo
True definition: a city in Mississippi
My definition: a cold temperature
Sentence: "The weatherman said it is going
to be *Tupelo* zero tonight!"

Word: Turanian
True definition: an Iranian-people settlement
My definition: weather-like conditions
Sentence: "We returned from a nice, sunny
vacation *Turanian*, windy weather back
home!"

Word: turf
True definition: the upper stratum of soil
bound by grass and plant roots
My definition: difficult to do or accomplish
Sentence: "The lawn-care man said he had a
turf job, but someone had to do it!"

Word: turnip
True definition: a vegetable
My definition: to increase volume

Smittionary
"Not your ordinary dictionary"
To get the best effect, say the italicized word(s) slowly

Sentence: "Tell him to please *turnip* the TV so we can hear the news!"

Word: Tuscaloosa
True definition: a city in Alabama
My definition: an untight ivory animal part
Sentence: "The large elephant's *Tuscaloosa* than the smaller elephant's tusk!"

Word: tutorship
True definition: the office, function, or work of a tutor
My definition: returning to a large boat
Sentence: "The navy officers were called back *tutorship* for a briefing!"

Word: tweak
True definition: to make small adjustments
My definition: lacking any strength
Sentence: "The skinny boy was *tweak* to carry the bricks and blocks!"

Word: twerk
True definition: a gyrating butt dance
My definition: place of employment
Sentence: "I can't go this weekend because I have *twerk* Saturday and Sunday!"

Smittionary
"Not your ordinary dictionary"
To get the best effect, say the italicized word(s) slowly

Word: twin

True definition: duplicate or match as

My definition: opposite of to lose

Sentence: "With that last score, it looks like they are going *twin* this game!"

Word: twine

True definition: a strong string made of two or more strands twisted together

My definition: treating a woman on a date

Sentence: "She is so nice, and I would love *twine* and dine her this weekend!"

Smittionary
"Not your ordinary dictionary"
To get the best effect, say the italicized word(s) slowly

U

Word: ultima
True definition: the last syllable of a word
My definition: giving due credit
Sentence: "This great fortune I have, I owe it *ultima* business associates!"

Word: ultimatum
True definition: a final proposition, condition, or demand
My definition: a suggestion to be introduced to someone
Sentence: "They are really nice people. You really *ultimatum* sometime!"

Word: unabated
True definition: being at full strength or force
My definition: a full fishing hook

Smittionary
"Not your ordinary dictionary"
To get the best effect, say the italicized word(s) slowly

Sentence: "The only way to catch fish is *unabated* fishing pole!"

Word: unadulterated
True definition: complete unqualified
My definition: classification such as a movie
Sentence: "You cannot have a PG-listing *unadulterated* R movies!"

Word: unappealing
True definition: not attractive
My definition: the pulled-off skin of fruit
Sentence: "She slipped and fell *unappealing* from a banana!"

Word: unassailable
True definition: not liable to doubt, attack, or question
My definition: a useable recreation vehicle
Sentence: "I won't buy anything nonworking, so I will only bid *unassailable* boat!"

Word: unaware
True definition: not knowing
My definition: destination questioning
Sentence: "*Unaware* do you think you are going, young man?"

Smittionary
"Not your ordinary dictionary"
To get the best effect, say the italicized word(s) slowly

Word: underemphasis

True definition: a reduced importance

My definition: a dictionary mistake for looking up the word *sis*

Sentence: "The dumb teacher said to check
the dictionary *underemphasis*, which
starts with an *s*."

Word: undermine

True definition: to subvert or weaken secretly

My definition: cosigning

Sentence: "Just sign your name *undermine*
next to the *X*!"

Word: underwrite

True definition: to set one's name to an insurance policy for liable losses

My definition: the opposite of looking left

Sentence: "The tour guide said, 'And *underwrite*,
you will see the beautiful state building!'"

Word: unique

True definition: being the only one or a distinct characteristic

My definition: to quietly surprise

Sentence: "I'm telling you, if *unique* up on
me like that again, I'm gonna hit you!"

Smittionary
"Not your ordinary dictionary"
To get the best effect, say the italicized word(s) slowly

Word: unit

True definition: a single quantity regarded as a whole in calculation

My definition: to interlace yarn or thread to make something

Sentence: "Hey, Cindy. I think *unit* better than you crochet!"

Word: united

True definition: relating to or produced by joint action

My definition: to honor for merit

Sentence: "I like the fact that *united* the worthy military man King Arthur!"

Word: *uno amino*

True definition: with one mind; unanimously

My definition: a request for additional work ethic

Sentence: "Now, Bob, *uno animo* work effort from you on this job to be successful!"

Word: untidy

True definition: not neat or messy

My definition: to free someone or something from restraint

Smittionary
"Not your ordinary dictionary"
To get the best effect, say the italicized word(s) slowly

Sentence: "Please go over there and *untidy* boat from the dock!"

Word: unto
True definition: used as a function word to indicate reference or concern
My definition: a counting toddler
Sentence: "We were all laughing as my son counted, saying, '*Unto,* fwee, four!'"

Word: upholster
True definition: to cover or fix with material
My definition: an oversized picture usually of an advertisement
Sentence: "My momma bought me *upholster* of my favorite singer!"

Word: uppity
True definition: arrogant
My definition: a shame
Sentence: "You know, it's *uppity* that they have no food"

Word: uraninite
True definition: a black mineral consisting of thorium and lead
My definition: a wet weather condition

Smittionary
"Not your ordinary dictionary"
To get the best effect, say the italicized word(s) slowly

Sentence: "Hey, it looks like *uraninite* has turned into a dry day today!"

Word: uremia
True definition: accumulation in the blood that can result in kidney disease
My definition: to recite words from a book
Sentence: "Hey, Mom, will *uremia* bedtime story before I go to sleep?"

Word: urine
True definition: liquid waste from the kidneys
My definition: a state of being or a location
Sentence: "Get ready, kid, 'cause *urine* the big leagues now!"

Word: urologist
True definition: a physician who specializes in the urinary tract
My definition: understanding positive intentions
Sentence: "I now see that *urologist* out here to have a good time!"

Word: useful
True definition: capable of being utilized
My definition: calling someone out
Sentence: "I hate saying this, but *useful* of crap!"

Smittionary
"Not your ordinary dictionary"
To get the best effect, say the italicized word(s) slowly

V

Word: vixen

True definition: a shrewish, ill-tempered woman

My definition: getting ready to

Sentence: "Please tell your brother that we are *vixen* to go!"

Smittionary
"Not your ordinary dictionary"
To get the best effect, say the italicized word(s) slowly

Word: waders

True definition: high waterproof boots used for fishing

My definition: food-service guys

Sentence: "This restaurant makes all the *waders* wear a tie!"

Word: wafer

True definition: a thin crisp cake, candy, or cracker

My definition: to determine poundage

Sentence: "On the fish scales, I need to *wafer* the correct weight!"

Word: wager

True definition: to place a bet

My definition: determined poundage of an item

Sentence: "I *wager* fish, and that is the correct weight!"

Smittionary
"Not your ordinary dictionary"
To get the best effect, say the italicized word(s) slowly

Word: Wahhabi

True definition: a member of a puritanical Muslim sect founded in Arabia

My definition: something that's uniquely enjoyable for you to do

Sentence: "He asked him, '*Wahhabi* are you working on now?'"

Word: Waikiki

True definition: resort section of Honolulu, Hawaii

My definition: questioning about a female friend

Sentence: "*Waikiki* can't go to the mall with us?"

Word: Waldo

True definition: a male name

My definition: the vertical separation sections of a house

Sentence: "He navigated the living room good, but he almost ran into that *Waldo*!"

Word: wallop

True definition: to hit with force

My definition: construction

Sentence: "The inside of the house will be done as soon as I get that last *wallop*!"

Smittionary
"Not your ordinary dictionary"
To get the best effect, say the italicized word(s) slowly

Word: Wannamaker

True definition: (John) a United States merchant and civic and religious leader

My definition: a lesson for others

Sentence: "The judge sentenced her to thirty years because he *Wannamaker* an example for future criminals."

Word: wannabee

True definition: a person that copies someone or something

My definition: a school-grade expectation

Sentence: "She received a C, but she really did *wannabe* in her science class!"

Word: warrior

True definition: a man experienced in warfare

My definition: clothing choice

Sentence: "I am so glad you *warrior* good dress tonight!"

Word: weaken

True definition: to make less strong

My definition: ability

Sentence: "I really think *weaken* make the trip in six hours!"

Smittionary
"Not your ordinary dictionary"
To get the best effect, say the italicized word(s) slowly

Word: weakish

True definition: somewhat not strong

My definition: lip-lock action

Sentence: "I lost count, but I think *weakish* for at least ten minutes!"

Word: weakling

True definition: one that is not strong in body, character, or mind

My definition: to stick closely to someone or something

Sentence: "The rescue worker said to make sure *weakling* to the mountain as best we can!"

Word: whammo

True definition: with violent abruptness

My definition: wardrobe choice

Sentence: "I've decided to *whammo* skirts and less pants to work!"

Word: whosoever

True definition: anyone included in an event or task

My definition: a clothes maker's claim

Sentence: "Just don't forget *whosoever* stitch of clothing you wear every day, young lady!"

Smittionary
"Not your ordinary dictionary"
To get the best effect, say the italicized word(s) slowly

Word: wigwam
True definition: an Indian hut
My definition: temperature control
Sentence: "Most women, to prevent cold heads,
     always wear a hat to keep their *wigwam*!"

Word: willow
True definition: a type of tree or shrub
My definition: lacking air
Sentence: "It looks like your left rear *willow*
     on air!"

Word: windowpane
True definition: a section of enclosed glass
My definition: relief from discomfort
Sentence: "I just had surgery, and I will be
     glad *windowpane* goes away for good!"

Word: winterize
True definition: to make ready for cold-weather
     season
My definition: to puff up or ascend
Sentence: "It's amazing how yeast rolls know
     winterize with a certain temperature!"

Word: wishy-washy
True definition: unable to stick to a decision

Smittionary
"Not your ordinary dictionary"
To get the best effect, say the italicized word(s) slowly

My definition: questions about a female

Sentence: "Four questions I need to know are *wishy-washy* could she be? Would she be?"

Word: wonton

True definition: a Chinese delicacy

My definition: a heavyweight

Sentence: "This vehicle weighs exactly *wonton* with the engine installed!"

Word: woodcutter

True definition: one who cuts wood

My definition: a bargain

Sentence: "After I called the car dealership for my daughter, the manager said they *woodcutter* a deal!"

Word: woodworker

True definition: a person skilled in making items from wood

My definition: annoyance

Sentence: "I knew all of those kids *woodworker* last nerve after a few hours!"

Word: Wyndham

True definition: (George) English poet and writer

Smittionary
"Not your ordinary dictionary"
To get the best effect, say the italicized word(s) slowly

My definition: victorious

Sentence: "After I saw the tennis tournament competition, I told my son he can *Wyndham* all!"

Smittionary
"Not your ordinary dictionary"
To get the best effect, say the italicized word(s) slowly

X

Word: x-ray
True definition: an internal photograph
My definition: a past-relationship person
Sentence: "It seems like everywhere she goes,
    she sees her *x-ray*!"

Smittionary
"Not your ordinary dictionary"
To get the best effect, say the italicized word(s) slowly

Y

Word: yacht
True definition: a large pleasure boat
My definition: a large quantity or quite a bit
Sentence: "They said the bachelor has a *yacht* going for him!"

First and Last Names That Shouldn't Go Together

If your last name is Andurny, don't name your
son Haybert.

If your last name is Hanson, don't name your
son Sanford.

If your last name is Wood or Durett, don't
name your son Sawyer.

If your last name is Jamison, don't name your
son Thaddeus.

If your last name is Wabbett, don't name your
daughter Celie.

If your last name is Pounder, don't name your
daughter Nell.

If your last name is Mater, don't name your
son Tom.

If your last name is Nader, don't name your
daughter Sarah.

If your last name is Curry, don't name your
daughter Kashon.

If your last name is Fants, don't name your
daughter Ellie.

If your last name is Meyers, don't name your
son Ed or Oscar.

If your last name is Purdy, don't name your
daughter Emma.

If your last name is Stinger, don't name your
son Herbic.

If your last name is Head, don't name your
daughter Lucinda.

If your last name is Sweat, don't name your
son Caesar.

If your last name is Quigley, don't name your daughter Mariam.

If your last name is Seville, don't name your daughter Barbara.

If your last name is Graham, don't name your son Teddy.

If your last name is Pope, don't name your daughter Frieda.

If your last name is Ball, don't name your daughter Havana.

If your last name is Shingles, don't name your daughter Ruth.

If your last name is Mint, don't name your son Horace.

If your last name is Bender, don't name your son Denny.

If your last name is Metcalf, don't name your son Butcher

If your last name is Ringer, don't name your
daughter Dora Bell.

If your last name is Wary, don't name your
son Don.

If your last name is Happy, don't name your
daughter Bea.

If your last name is Rainey, don't name your
daughter Wendy.

If your last name is Bugg, don't name your
daughter Lita.

If your last name is Dunnett, don't name your
son Hugh.

If your last name is Dorsett, don't name your
son E. C.

If your last name is Artest, don't name your
son Akon.

If your last name is Dover, don't name your
son Enoch.

If your last name is Case, don't name your son Curt.

If your last name is Fender, don't name your son Denton.

If your last name is Walken, don't name your daughter Abby.

If your last name is Burns, don't name your son Sonnie.

If your last name is Dottie, don't name your daughter Lottie.

If your last name is Moss, don't name your son Pete.

If your last name is Plummer, don't name your daughter Anita.

If your last name is Woods, don't name your daughter Holly or your son Baron.

If your last name is Tilly, don't name your son Yuto.

If your last name is Titer, don't name your daughter Lucy.

If your last name is Tingham, don't name your son Tex.

If your last name is Knack, don't name your son Nick.

If your last name is Oliver, don't name your son Earl.

If your last name is Marker, don't name your daughter Amiya.

If your last name is Whitehead, don't name your son Buster.

If your last name is Poole, don't name your son Gene.

If your last name is Deplain, don't name your daughter Maryland.

If your last name is Forrest, don't name your daughter Carmen.

If your last name is Waters, don't name your daughter Flo.

If your last name is Katz, don't name your daughter Allie.

If your last name is Mills, don't name your son Eaton.

If your last name is McCoy, don't name your daughter Ariel.

If your last name is Pugh, don't name your son Ishmael.

If your last name is Spellman, don't name your son Edward.

If your last name is King, don't name your daughter May.

If your last name is Banks, don't name your daughter Robin.

If your last name is Runner, don't name your son Walker.

If your last name is Steele, don't name your son Obie.

If your last name is Woodson, don't name your son Chuck.

If your last name is Fishman, don't name your son Yusef.

If your last name is Sumpton, don't name your daughter Taylor.

If your last name is Touett, don't name your son Adam.

If your last name is Conns, don't name your daughter Frieda.

If your last name is Rigger, don't name your son Orwell.

If your last name is Manson, don't name your daughter Hilda.

If your last name is Finns, don't name your daughter Dee.

If your last name is Seacup, don't name your son Maurice.

If your last name is Downs, don't name your son Marcus.

If your last name is Barley, don't name your son Wheaton.

If your last name is Short, don't name your daughter Penny.

If your last name is Miles, don't name your son Randy.

If your last name is Able, don't name your son Canaan.

If your last name is Bust, don't name your daughter Misty.

If your last name is Addle, don't name your daughter Missy.

If your last name is Haven, don't name your daughter Miss Bea.

If your last name is Goode, don't name your daughter Emma.

If your last name is Heckler, don't name your daughter Ima.

If your last name is Bowie, don't name your daughter Etta.

If your last name is Mann, don't name your son Dwight.

If your last name is Pance, don't name your son Marty.

If your last name is Mudder, don't name your son Foster.

If your last name is Carr, don't name your daughter Lisa.

If your last name is Ford or Back, don't name your twin daughters Eileen and Eulene.

If your last name is Reddy, don't name your daughter Summer.

If your last name is Dunn, don't name your daughter Gladys.

If your last name is Springs, don't name your son Lief.

If your last name is Toomer, don't name your son Fount.

If your last name is Rivers, don't name your daughter Flo.

If your last name is Wall, don't name your son Walter.

If your last name is Malone, don't name your daughter Aleva.

If your last name is Bayer, don't name your daughter Athena.

If your last name is Payne, don't name your daughter Ophelia.

If your last name is Baker, don't name your daughter Candi.

If your last name is Riser, don't name your son Earl E.

If your last name is Leaseman, don't name your son Paul.

If your last name is Anderson, don't name your son Herman.

If your last name is Witherspoon, don't name your daughter Akila.

If your last name is Bell, don't name your daughter Dora.

If your last name is Cooper, don't name your daughter Minnie.

If your last name is Foote, don't name your son Tony.

If your last name is Sunnie, don't name your son Brighton.

If your last name is Hyde, don't name your son Tanner.

If your last name is Pincher, don't name your son Willie.

If your last name is Ryder, don't name your son DeCarlo.

If your last name is Sheppard, don't name your son Jermaine.

If your last name is Back, don't name your daughter Carmen.

If your last name is Tuller, don't name your son Tito.

If your last name is Knott, don't name your daughter Phyllis.

If your last name is Dover, don't name your twin girls Eileen and Eulene.

If your last name is Lott, don't name your daughter Eliza.

If your last name is Durrett, don't name your twins Al and Will.

If your last name is Locks, don't name your son Jimmy.

If your last name is Toll, don't name your son Jerry.

If your last name is Pickens, don't name your son Barry or Slim.

If your last name is Winns, don't name your daughter Suzanne.

If your last name is Money, don't name your daughter Linda.

If your last name is Buster, don't name your son Phillip.

If your last name is Moore, don't name your son Manny.

If your last name is Atlas, don't name your son Humphrey.

If your last name is Brewer, don't name your son Artie.

If your last name is Dings, don't name your son Bill.

If your last name is Weathers, don't name your twins Sonny and Wendy.

If your last name is James, don't name your son Eric.

If your last name is Adder, don't name your daughter Ima.

If your last name is Turner, don't name your son Will.

If your last name is Sheralike, don't name your daughter Sharon.

If your last name is Graffer, don't name your son Otto.

If your last name is Day, don't name your daughter Hallie.

If your last name is Singer, don't name your daughter Carol.

If your last name is Bush, don't name your
daughter Rose.

If your last name is Duett, don't name your
daughter Mamie.

If your last name is Dover, don't name your
son Ben.

If your last name is Miles, don't name your
daughter Minnie.

If your last name is Garrett, don't name your
son Mack.

If your last name is Dunn, don't name your
son Ben.

If your last name is Hunt, don't name your
son Willie.

If your last name is Banks, don't name your
son Rob.

If your last name is Moore, don't name your
daughter Annie.

If your last name is Weyer, don't name your daughter Barb.

If your last name is Ficks, don't name your daughter Anita.

If your last name is Case, don't name your son Justin.

If your last name is Foyer, don't name your daughter Carmen.

If your last name is Whack, don't name your daughter Pattie.

If your last name is Taylor, don't name your daughter Ima.

If your last name is Hand, don't name your daughter Linda.

If your last name is Dow, don't name your son Howard.

If your last name is Ennoy, don't name your son Earl.

If your last name is Pade, don't name your son Bill.

If your last name is Setgoe, don't name your son Mark.

If your last name is Ayzonn, don't name your son Lee.

If your last name is Graham, don't name your daughter Polly.

If your last name is Bates, don't name your daughter Dee.

If your last name is Klair, don't name your daughter Ida.

If your last name is Wood, don't name your son Sawyer.

If your last name is Wannah, don't name your daughter Mary.

If your last name is Tabels, don't name your son Trey.

If your last name is Byrd, don't name your son Jay.

If your last name is Hobba, don't name your daughter Pearl.

If your last name is Mentory, don't name your son Rudy.

If your last name is King, don't name your son Joe.

If your last name is Lize, don't name your daughter Pearl.

If your last name is Paw, don't name your son Paul.

If your last name is Hertz, don't name your son Herbert.

If your last name is Dice, don't name your son Chip.

If your last name is Trephick, don't name your daughter Alana.

If your last name it Mettick, don't name your
son Otto.

If your last name is Land, don name your
daughter Ima Tilda.

If your last name is Ess, don't name your
daughter Ira.

If your last name is Wunanatoo, don't name
your daughter Anna.

If your last name is Able, don't name your son
Canaan.

If your last name is Arms, don't name your
son Dakota.

If your last name is Picker, don't name your
son Barry.

If your last name is Meenott, don't name your
daughter Sheila.

If your last name is Toste, don't name your
son Burt.

If your last name is Reetheef, don't name your daughter Jewel.

If your last name is Uhlantin, don't name your son Jack.

If your last name is Daze, don't name your daughter Holly.

If your last name is Reeder, don't name your son Chip.

If your last name is Absent, don't name your son Marcus.

If your last name is Keeyoot, don't name your son Percy.

If your last name is Pance, don't name your son Peter.

If your last name is Arnotobee, don't name your son Toby.

If your last name is Graws, don't name your son Marty.

If your last name is Tocks, don't name your son Burt.

If your last name is Peeples, don't name your daughter Hilda.

If your last name is Fullafeesh, don't name your daughter Annette.

If your last name is Lean, don't name your daughter Mabel.

If your last name is Ensense, don't name your son Frank.

If your last name is Bubbles, don't name your son Pablo.

If your last name is Sawft, don't name your daughter Angel.

If your last name is Tuckett, don't name your son Paul.

If your last name is Wannitt, don't name your son Don.

If your last name is Tewth, don't name your son Chip.

If your last name is Yoobeeweebee, don't name your daughter Abby.

If your last name is Ringer, don't name your daughter Abella.

If your last name is Insunn, don't name your son Tucker.

If your last name is Coates, don't name your daughter Patty.

If your last name is Ratt, don't name your son Jim.

If your last name is Rock, don't name your daughter Pat.

If your last name is Gaiter, don't name your daughter Allie.

If your last name is Tanks, don't name your son Sherman.

If your last name is Scotting, don't name your
son Wayne.

If your last name is Peach, don't name your
daughter Aida.

If your last name is Babba, don't name your
daughter Allie.

If your last name is Motter, don't name your
daughter Alma.

If your last name is Cooke, don't name your
daughter Amelia.

If your last name is Rings, don't name your
daughter Annabel.

If your last name is Tubbs, don't name your
daughter Annabeth.

If your last name is Toast, don't name your
daughter Bernadette.

If your last name is Benz, don't name your
daughter Bethany.

If your last name is Lyon, don't name your daughter Betty.

If your last name is Overwater, don't name your daughter Bridgette.

If your last name is Flowing, don't name your daughter Brooke.

If your last name is Fornya, don't name your daughter Callie.

If your last name is Ghettit, don't name your daughter Carmen.

If your last name is Fate, don't name your daughter Celia.

If your last name is Money, don't name your daughter Cindy.

If your last name is Voyant, don't name your daughter Claire.

If your last name is Barr, don't name your daughter Clarke.

If your last name is Pebbles, don't name your daughter Coco.

If your last name is Oskopee, don't name your son Colin.

If your last name is Call, don't name your daughter Collette.

If your last name is Paint, don't name your son Dakota.

If your last name is Allott, don't name your daughter Danielle.

If your last name is Finns, don't name your daughter Dee.

If your last name is Andaneffew, don't name your daughter Dennise.

If your last name is Endaruff, don't name your daughter Diamond.

If your last name is Jainenspot, don't name your daughter Dixie.

If your last name is Opinned, don't name your daughter Doris.

If your last name is Allup, don't name your daughter Edith.

If your last name is Peese, don't name your son Warren.

If your last name is Meegoode, don't name your daughter Egypt.

If your last name is Menopee, don't name your daughter Ella.

If your last name is Getnoowons, don't name your daughter Emerald.

If your last name is Reelgoode, don't name your daughter Emma.

If your last name is Notbiskits, don't name your daughter Emma Rose.

If your last name is Jockwa, don't name your daughter Farrah.

If your last name is Goe, don't name your daughter Frieda.

If your last name is Dajungol, don't name your daughter Georgia.

If your last name is Nottmee, don't name your daughter Gladys.

If your last name is Meehertz, don't name your daughter Autumn.

If your last name is Dakradel, don't name your daughter Robin.

If your last name is Loxx, don't name your daughter Goldie.

If your last name is Davison, don't name your daughter Harlee.

If your last name is Gritz, don't name your daughter Harmony.

If your last name is Upp, don't name your daughter Harriet.

If your last name is Ball, don't name your daughter Havana.

If your last name is Wutsup, don't name your daughter Haylee.

If your last name is Ho, don't name your daughter Heidi.

If your last name is Back, don't name your daughter Helen.

If your last name is Jolly, don't name your daughter Holly.

If your last name is Klamp, don't name your daughter Hosanna.

If your last name is Ho, don't name your daughter Ida.

If your last name is Yoreland, don't name your daughter Ireland.

If your last name is Itall, don't name your daughter Iris.

If your last name is Trust, don't name your
daughter Irma.

If your last name is Kloser, don't name your
daughter Isadora.

If your last name is Day, don't name your
daughter Ivory.

If your last name is Fluid, don't name your
daughter Ivy.

If your last name is Hyde, don't name your
daughter Jacqueline.

If your last name is Torr, don't name your
daughter Jana.

If your last name is Playsongs, don't name
your daughter Jasmine.

If your last name is Poole, don't name your
daughter Jean.

If your last name is Camalla, don't name your
daughter Joanne.

If your last name is Dover, don't name your
daughter Jolene.

If your last name is Anpayne, don't name your
daughter Joy.

If your last name is Whutt, don't name your
daughter Juno.

If your last name is Wunce, don't name your
daughter Justice.

If your last name is Njojo, don't name your
daughter Kasey.

If your last name is Boutcha, don't name your
daughter Karen.

If your last name is Ova, don't name your
daughter Katalina.

If your last name is Passaklass, don't name
your daughter Kennedy.

If your last name is Pheelitt, don't name your
daughter Kenya.

If your last name is Inhardee, don't name your
daughter Laurel.

If your last name is Leggett, don't name your
daughter Toni.

If your last name is Onmeeya, don't name
your daughter Lena.

If your last name is Ondalaybol, don't name
your daughter Libby.

If your last name is Lott, don't name your
daughter Liza.

If your last name is Bridges, don't name your
daughter London.

If your last name is Ticks, don't name your
daughter Luna.

If your last name is Astrike, don't name your
daughter Mabel.

If your last name is Meeaginn, don't name
your daughter Macie.

If your last name is Kingluv, don't name your daughter Mae.

If your last name is Hertz, don't name your daughter Maria.

If your last name is Knott, don't name your daughter May.

If your last name is Yooah, don't name your daughter Mia.

If your last name is Meeheer, don't name your daughter Millicent.

If your last name is Ishott, don't name your daughter Minerva.

If your last name is Lott, don't name your daughter Mona.

If your last name is Dabote, don't name your son Monroe.

If your last name is Gailswant, don't name your daughter Amanda.

If your last name is Money, don't name your
daughter Naomi.

If your last name is Slaw, don't name your
daughter Nicole.

If your last name is Mann, don't name your
son Noah.

If your last name is Cee, don't name your
daughter Norma.

If your last name is Shame, don't name your
daughter Odessa.

If your last name is Heer, don't name your
daughter Olive.

If your last name is Payne, don't name your
daughter Ophelia.

If your last name is Turner, don't name your
daughter Paige.

If your last name is Carr, don't name your son
Parker.

If your last name is Ticks, don't name your daughter Paula.

If your last name is Meegoe, don't name your daughter Paulette.

If your last name is Place, don't name your daughter Payton.

If your last name is Lize, don't name your daughter Pearl.

If your last name is Urned, don't name your daughter Penny.

If your last name is High, don't name your daughter Phoebe.

If your last name is Onhisself, don't name your daughter Poppy.

If your last name is Lawd, don't name your daughter Precious.

If your last name is Mee, don't name your daughter Rae.

If your last name is Madd, don't name your
daughter Raven.

If your last name is Eecupp, don't name your
daughter Reese.

If your last name is Tooley, don't name your
daughter Rhetta.

If your last name is Booke, don't name your
daughter Rita.

If your last name is Dakradel, don't name
your daughter Robin.

If your last name is ArRed, don't name your
daughter Rosa.

If your last name is DaMann, don't name
your daughter Rosemary.

If your last name is Boulders, don't name your
daughter Roxanne.

If your last name is Redd, don't name your
daughter Ruby.

If your last name is Wurds, don't name your daughter Sadie.

If your last name is Tahoe, don't name your daughter Sahara.

If your last name is Wabbitt, don't name your daughter Sally.

If your last name is Beeches, don't name your daughter Sandy.

If your last name is Nader, don't name your daughter Sarah.

If your last name is Squatch, don't name your daughter Sasha.

If your last name is Wood, don't name your son Sawyer.

If your last name is Uvitt, don't name your daughter Shannon.

If your last name is Sheralike, don't name your daughter Sharon.

If your last name is Heersoon, don't name your daughter Shelby.

If your last name is Mistakin, don't name your daughter Shirley.

If your last name is Aseecrat, don't name your daughter Tammy.

If your last name is Issa-Opin, don't name your daughter Theadora.

If your last name is Headhertz, don't name your daughter Uma.

If your last name is Upponemm, don't name your daughter Unique.

If your last name is Arrbloo, don't name your daughter Violet.

If your last name is Daze, don't name your daughter Wendy.

If your last name is Onnaire, don't name your daughter Willow.

If your last name is Roast, don't name your daughter Winnie.

If your last name is Boddeed, don't name your son Abel.

If your last name is Hock, don't name your son Abraham.

If your last name is Buggs, don't name your son Achilles.

If your last name is Scores, don't name your son Andy.

If your last name is Benz, don't name your son Anthony.

If your last name is Ree. Don't name your son Archer.

If your last name is Day, don't name your son Avery.

If your last name is Weevoll, don't name your son Beau.

If your name is Derrdundatt, don't name your son Ben.

If your last name is Over, don't name your son Benjamin.

If your last name is Tater, don't name your son Benedict.

If your last name is Entoshape, don't name your son Benjamin.

If your last name is Gotes, don't name your son Billy.

If your last name is Naler, don't name your son Brad.

If your last name is Hare, don't name your son Braden.

If your last name is Bonch, don't name your son Brady.

If your last name is Pack, don't name your son Brett.

If your last name is Aroni, don't name your son Brice.

If your last name is Ohbahmah, don't name your son Brock.

If your last name is Coffey or Tee, don't name your son Bruno.

If your last name is Durr, don't name your son Callen.

If your last name is Walker, don't name your son Canaan.

If your last name is Lott, don't name your son Carl.

If your last name is Toodaground, don't name your son Carlo.

If your last name is Notyores, don't name your son Carmine.

If your last name is Uvmeets, don't name your son Carver.

If your last name is Clowes, don't name your sone Case.

If your last name is Enjojo, don't name your son Casey.

If your last name is Munnee, don't name your son Cassius.

If your last name is Bubes, don't name your son Cesar.

If your last name is Tuwinn, don't name your son Chance.

If your last name is Yurdreem, don't name your son Chase.

If your last name is Peabakin, don't name your son Chris.

If your last name is Barr, don't name your son Clark.

If your last name is Potts, don't name your son Clay.

If your last name is Hanger, don't name your son Cliff.

If your last name is Fender, don't name your son Cody.

If your last name is Tuwerk, don't name your son Collin.

If your last name is Aygerr, don't name your son Constantine.

If your last name is Chikkens, don't name your son Cooper.

If your last name is Tuss, don't name your son Coy.

If your last name is Mengell, don't name your son Cristian.

If your last name is Bing, don't name your son Crosby.

If your last name is Kuntroll, don't name your son Cruz.

If your last name is Narry, don't name your
son Cullen.

If your last name is Arms or Paynt, don't name
your son Dakota.

If your last name is Goodsope, don't name
your son Dallas.

If your last name is Andalegg, don't name
your son Danny.

If your last name is McCoy, don't name your
son Dario.

If your last name is Andhammer, don't name
your son Darnell.

If your last name Issblowinn, don't name your
son Darwin.

If your last name is Uhgurl, don't name your
son Dayton.

If your last name is Saxxon, don't name your
son Deangelo.

If your last name is Polowe, don't name your son Demarco.

If your last name is Mytess, don't name your son Deon.

If your last name is Halls, don't name your son Dexter.

If your last name is Witchew, don't name your son Dillon.

If your last name is Byter, don't name your son Donnell.

If your last name is Fildmore, don't name your son Douglas.

If your last name is Dafurniture, don't name your son Dustin.

If your last name is Andadawter, don't name your son Edison.

If your last name is Tumuch, don't name your son Eli.

If your last name is Afterkay, don't name your son Ellis.

If your last name is Mammacooked, don't name your son Emilio.

If your last name is Lovecheese, don't name your son Everette.

If your last name is Uvmenn, don't name your son Fisher.

If your last name is Akuntree, don't name your son Francis.

If your last name is Furrter, don't name your son Frank.

If your last name is Knott, don't name your son Fred.

If your last name is Papers, don't name your son Grady.

If your last name is Uvcoak, don't name your son Graham.

If your last name is Notbloo, don't name your son Grayson.

If your last name is Zerr, don't name your son Guy.

If your last name is Keypankee, don't name your son Hank.

If your last name is Mann, don't name your son Harold.

If your last name is Nappee, don't name your son Harris.

If your last name is Mint, don't name your son Harris.

If your last name is Back, don't name your son Harry.

If your last name is Cheets, don't name your son Herman.

If your last name is Onn, don't name your son Holden.

If your last name is Baye, don't name your son Hudson.

If your last name is Dattaway, don't name your son Hugo.

If your last name is Uvgame, don't name your son Hunter.

If your last name is Jaybrandey, don't name your son Ian.

If your last name is Boyee, don't name your son Isaiah.

If your last name is Handol, don't name your son Jack.

If your last name is Izgroan, don't name your son Jamison.

If your last name is Byrd, don't name your son Jay.

If your last name is Sheppard, don't name your son Jermaine.

If your last name is Manderer, don't name your son Jerry.

If your last name is Rivers, don't name your son Jordan.

If your last name is Inwitcha, don't name your son Josh.

If your last name is Mowtime, don't name your son Juan.

If your last name is Survd, don't name your son Justice.

If your last name is Walsh, don't name your son Karl.

If your last name is Punchen, don't name your son Kyle.

If your last name is Alott, don't name your son Lance.

If your last name is Daplain, don't name your son Landon.

If your last name is Tardee, don't name your son Layton.

If your last name is Blower, don't name your son Lief.

If your last name is Clausett, don't name your son Lennon.

If your last name is Engton, don't name your son Lex.

If your last name is Loggs, don't name your son Lincoln.

If your last name is Upp, don't name your son Linus.

If your last name is Hammercy, don't name your son Lloyd.

If your last name is Bridges, don't name your son London.

If your last name is Wutyadid, don't name your son Luciano.

If your last name is Heera, don't name your son Luka.

If your last name is Anthwinner, don't name your son Luther.

If your last name is Ahann, don't name your son Lyndon.

If your last name is Meelater, don't name your son Macy.

If your last name is Itzshoaz, don't name your son Madden.

If your last name is Keyfawsitt, don't name your son Malik.

If your last name is Moore, don't name your son Manny.

If your last name is Layboar, don't name your son Manuel.

If your last name is Mywurds, don't name your son Marc.

If your last name is Present, don't name your son Marcus.

If your last name is Daddee, don't name your son Mario.

If your last name is Joseph, don't name your son Marion.

If your last name is Hurtz, don't name your son Mateo.

If your last name is Izzhizzname, don't name your son Maverick.

If your last name is Trux, don't name your son Max.

If your last name is Ankollee don't name your son Mel.

If your last name is Friend, don't name your son Miguel.

If your last name is Stand, don't name your son Mike.

If your last name is Toogoe, don't name your son Miles.

If your last name is Ryder, don't name your son Milo.

If your last name is Snow, don't name your son Milton.

If your last name is Lass, don't name your son Morris.

If your last name is Carrlow, don't name your son Monty.

If your last name is Inguvteeth, don't name your son Nash.

If your last name is Ensite, don't name your son Nolan.

If your last name is Alott, don't name your son Oliver.

If your last name is Garsh, don't name your son Omar.

If your last name is Meyers, don't name your
son Oscar.

If your last name is Aintmine, don't name
your son Otis.

If your last name is Mettick, don't name your
son Otto.

If your last name is Peeple, don't name your
son Owen.

If your last name is Bubbolls, don't name your
son Pablo.

If your last name is Rheer, don't name your
son Palmer.

If your last name is Carr, don't name your son
Parker.

If your last name is Lathor, don't name your
son Patton.

If your last name is Engears, don't name your
son Pearce.

If your last name is Pance, don't name your son Peter.

If your last name is Dacarr, don't name your son Phillip.

If your last name is Tuppletts, don't name your son Quinn.

If your last name is Down, don't name your son Raphael.

If your last name is Jingbull, don't name your son Ray.

If your last name is Seecups, don't name your son Reese.

If your last name is Abooke, don't name your son Reed.

If your last name is Trapp, don't name your son Rhett.

If your last name is Flose, don't name your son River.

If your last name is Roundahouse, don't name your son Rocco.

If your last name is Rhodes, don't name your son Rocky.

If your last name is Datt, don't name your son Roger.

If your last name is Ondarever, don't name your son Roland.

If your last name is Charges, don't name your son Roman.

If your last name is Verr, don't name your son Romeo.

If your last name is Payne, don't name your son or daughter Royal.

If your last name is Ling, don't name your son Russell.

If your last name is Truxx, don't name your son Ryder.

If your last name is Eyeyam, don't name your son Sam.

If your last name is Mahmah, don't name your son Sawyer.

If your last name is Daloid, don't name your son Seth.

If your last name is Mommetter, don't name your son Therm.

If your last name is Knobbs, don't name your son Theodore.

If your last name is Lewsin, don't name your son Titan.

If your last name is Hertin, don't name your son Toby.

If your last name is Lerrs, don't name your son Todd.

If your last name is Gunns, don't name your son Tommy.

If your last name is Andternin, don't name your son Tristan.

If your last name is Enn, don't name your son Tucker.

If your last name is Ohverr, don't name your son Turner.

If your last name is Uhnott, don't name your son Ty.

If your last name is Cheekin, don't name your son Tyson.

If your last name is Seetzmee, don't name your son Usher.

If your last name is Tastik, don't name your son Van.

If your last name is Rhees, don't name your son Victor.

If your last name is Dahbeel, don't name your son Vito.

If your last name is Dingpool, don't name your son Wade.

If your last name is Runner, don't name your son Walker.

If your last name is Paynted, don't name your son Wallace.

If your last name is Peece, don't name your son Warren.

If your last name is Likeabaybee, don't name your son Waylon.

If your last name is Turns, don't name your son Wes.

If your last name is Kyotee, don't name your son Wiley.

If your last name is Barroes, don't name your son Will.

If your last name is Andeelem, don't name your son Willem.

If your last name is Gottabeedissway, don't name your son Wyatt.

If your last name is Izfree, don't name your son Yamil.

If your last name is Kuh, don't name your son Yuri.

If your last name is Dahpu, don't name your daughter Winnie.

Cannibal Jokes

Cannibals like their eggs "ovaries Z."

A cannibal-owned pizza place sign in the window: We "de-liver."

A cannibal spotted a dog and got excited and said, "Hey... A Quarter 'Hound-er' with 'Fleas!'"

Two cannibals were watching *The Wizard of Oz* and kept rewinding to the songs, "If I Only Had a Brain" and "If I Only Had a Heart!"

Two cannibals went to one of their restaurants and ordered food. The cashier asked them, "Do you want flies with that?"

A cannibal was eating someone's belly and said, "I'm working on a full stomach!"

Some cannibals are auditioning for a new TV show called "Deface the Nation!!"

A cannibal's wife proudly announces, "For dinner, we gonna have a shoulder roast!"

One cannibal said, "I can't believe I ate the whole thing!"
Another one said, "Yes… You ate Ralph!"

One of the victims pulled out a gun and was going to shoot until the cannibal "disarmed" him!

Cannibals water at the mouth when someone says, "I stuck my foot in my mouth again!"

A reporter asked one cannibal if he did not think he was going to get caught. The cannibal said, "It was worth the 'wrist!'"

Two cannibals went to a party, and one of them said, "This party sucks… All they have is finger food!"

A cannibal said to the other, "Man, I'm hungry… Watch me as 'Achilles' ribs!"

One cannibal asked the other one, "You want a knuckle sandwich?"

One cannibal asked the other one, "Hey! What kind of 'colon' are you wearing?"

The cannibal that ate the brain wanted a good "souse" of nutrition…brain food!

A cannibal was eating someone's face, and all of a sudden, he had to sneeze…"Eye chew!"

A cannibal was eating a foot… He "toe" that "sole" food up!"

A cannibal saw Siamese twins and said, "Great…a two-for-one special today!"

Four cannibals went to a football game and looked at the crowd, and one of them said, "Great! An all-you-can-eat restaurant!"

A cannibal went to the doctor, and the doctor told him he had tennis elbow! The cannibal said, "How do you know what I had for lunch?"

A third cannibal was eating a detached ear,
 and the victim could hear him chewing!

Another cannibal was eating someone's face,
 and he spit the eyes out... He did not
 like "see food!"

About the Author

 Meet Timothy "Smitty" Smith, born and raised in Lexington, Kentucky, and has been a jokester since childhood. He is married, a father with one daughter, and he has three siblings. Both of his parents are deceased but they had a positive impact on his life.

While enjoying retirement, he loves making people laugh with his "punny" and "play on words" style of humor. He has authored another book titled *For a Pun Time Call Smitty* that's a combination of "yo mama/family jokes," "bad pickup lines," and miscellaneous "play on words" jokes that is currently available at Amazon.com, Barnesandnoble.com, and many other major bookstores nationwide. Along with being an author, he is also an inventor with a United States Patent in his name granted by Toyota Motor Engineering and Manufacturing, which is his previous employer (US Patent 8080745, patents. google.com/patent/US8080745B2/en).

He currently resides in Louisville, Kentucky, with his wife of twenty-four years and enjoys family time, bicycling, and tinkering in his spare time.